Application of Systems Thinking Ontologies to Develop a Multi-Dimensional Strategy Model

A Research Report
by
Jimmy Brown, Ph.D.

Application of Systems Thinking Ontologies to Develop a Multi-Dimensional Strategy Model

Copyright © 2009 by Jimmy Brown, Ph.D.

Contents based upon *Doctoral Dissertation Leveraging an OD Perspective to Develop a New Model of Strategy Formulation*, Copyright © 2007 by Jimmy Brown

All rights reserved. No part of this book may be used or reproduced by any means, graphic, electronic, or mechanical, including photocopying, recording, taping or by any information storage retrieval system without the written permission of the author except in the case of brief quotations embodied in critical articles and reviews, or with appropriate citations in scholarly work.

Copies may be ordered through booksellers or by contacting:
Jimmy Brown, Ph.D.
www.3cstrategy.com
www.jimmybrownphd.com

Because of the dynamic nature of the Internet, any Web addresses or links contained in this book may have changed since publication and may no longer be valid.

ISBN: 978-1449957162 (sc)

Printed in the United States of America

Executive Summary

What are the unique aspects of a given organization that enable it outperform its rivals? Is it superior products? Is it a better service model? Is it some combination of the two? Is it merely a matter of aligning the organization's product and service offerings with the needs of the market place at a particular time? Strategy is about finding ways for organizations to answer these questions in order to create sustainable competitive advantage (Hamel, 1996; Porter, 1996; Worley et al., 1996). Recently, however, there has been a realization that the current strategy paradigms have failed to consistently live up to their potential, and as a result, there have been calls to revisit the predominant models and approaches used in this process (Collis & Montgomery, 1995; Cummings & Angwin, 2004; Mintzberg, 1994). This report describes research that attempts to respond to those calls by applying a systems thinking lens to the current strategy formulation ontologies to develop a new model that addresses some of the criticisms of the major strategy formulation paradigms. This challenge was undertaken by answering the following research question:

Do organizations that take an approach to strategy formulation that is consistent with a model based on a systems thinking perspective perform better than the overall market?

The efforts to answer this question began with the development of the Multi-Dimensional Strategy Model (MDSM). This new model was tested by submitting a strategy-formulation questionnaire to top-performing organizations, and then using those responses to determine the degree to which the proposed MDSM reflected reality. The results indicate that this model does indeed represent how top performing organizations go about their strategy formulation processes. Moreover, the responses indicate that the participants do view their strategy formulation processes as having a positive impact on their organizations' performance. This suggests that the MDSM could have a positive impact on the performance of organizations that chose to use it. In addition, the same system thinking lens was also applied to analyzing how these organizations make sense of the various kinds of data that they incorporate into their strategy formulation efforts. These insights were then integrated into the MDSM to extend the understanding of the strategy formulation process, and answer the calls for new thinking in this arena.

The new thinking that was developed during this study is useful because it clearly defines the assumptions and generalizations that managers need to take into account when incorporating capabilities, customers, and competition into their strategy formulation processes. This new thinking also illustrates that top performing organizations make sense of all those different kinds of data by understanding their own organizational orientations, which allows the managers to select the data elements and decision techniques that best meet each organization's unique needs. While there is still work that could be done in this line of research, the outcomes of this study suggest that the application of a systems thinking perspective does enable organizations to integrate these multiple perspectives into their strategy processes, and make appropriate sense of those disparate data points. Both of which were shown here to be key drivers of organizational success.

Table of Contents

Executive Summary v
Table of Contents ix
Introduction 11
Theoretical Background 13
   An Overview of Strategy 13
   Strategy as an Organization Responding to Its Environment 17
   Strategy as an Organization Leveraging Core Capabilities 20
   The Evolving Customer Management Paradigm 23
   An Eye Towards an Integrated Model 27
Research Methods 35
   Research Design 35
   Quantitative Phase 37
   Qualitative Phase 43
   Questionnaire Development 45
   Participant Selection 50
   Data Collection 54
Data Analysis & Results 59
   Sample Representativeness 59
   Quantitative Analysis & Results 64
   Qualitative Analysis & Results 71
      Q_1: Competitor Information in the Strategy Formulation Process 75
      Q_2: Capability Information in the Strategy Formulation Process 80
      Q_3: Customer Information in the Strategy Formulation Process 85
      Q_4: Sense-making in the Strategy Formulation Process 89
   Finalized Multi-Dimensional Strategy Model 98
Implications & Application 101
List of Figures 105
List of Tables 107
References 109
About the Author 115

Introduction

Simply put, this book is a research report. Similar to works like *Good to Great* and *In Search of Excellence*, it is an effort to express the findings of a rigorous scholarly study. The particular study in this case was a doctoral dissertation. Like any doctoral dissertation, the original write-up included lots of verbose language and excruciating detail. The intent of that effort was to convince a committee of Ph.D.s that the author was competent to conduct independent research.

The goal of this endeavor is to summarize the efforts and outcomes of that study so that they may be appreciated by slightly wider audiences. The intended audiences are the study participants and other scholars who may be interested in leveraging similar ontologies and/or methodologies at some later date. As such, it is fully expected that some readers may still find the terminology and style to be somewhat *dissertationish*. It is therefore fully expected that this text will appeal to a fairly small audience, but mass marketing of this particular version is not the objective.

The objective is to review the short comings of the current strategic planning ontologies and offer recommendations for addressing them. Strategic planning of is keen interest to business leaders today, not just because of its impact on business outcomes, but also because a lot of people think it is *really really cool*. Ask anyone who conducts job interviews and they will likely agree that the most common strength that candidates express about themselves is "the ability to think strategically."

As important as that ability is, thinking strategically and strategic planning are two completely different things. Strategic thinking is a way of looking at something from beginning to end and being able to understand all the interdependencies and potential outcomes (Leath, 2007). Strategic planning on the other hand is a process through which some organizations make high level plans to achieve desired outcomes over a particular period of time. Ironically, it is often a lack of strategic thinking that leads to a failure to realize the goals described in strategic plans. This book offers some suggestions on how to address those deficiencies by providing insights on how to apply a particular kind of strategic thinking known as *systems theory* to the strategic planning process. It not only describes the theoretical basis for this assertion but also reports real world data that demonstrates that many top performing organizations are already applying these kinds of mental models, even if they do not formally realize it.

Theoretical Background

An Overview of Strategy

What is strategy? That question is regularly explored in both theory and practice, and the answer serves as a guide post to many of the subsequent actions that organizations take. The term comes from the Greek word *strategos* and loosely translated means *art of the general* (Collis, 2005). The Chinese military philosopher Sun Tzu said that the responsibility of generalship is to create situations that assure victory (Griffith, 1963). Following this line of thinking, it would be possible to conceptualize strategy as an approach for creating situations that allow organizations to be successful. While there have been numerous variations on this theme throughout the study of the phenomenon (Hamel & Prahalad, 1989; Porter, 1996; Worley et al., 1996), it is possible to amalgamate the various definitions into a single conceptualization; such as, the intent of strategy is to create sustainable competitive advantage that allows organizations to outperform their competitors over time, even in the face of changing environments.

No one would challenge the notion that achieving competitive advantage over competitors is good idea, but the number of organizations that fail every year to do just that makes it obvious that accomplishing this goal is very difficult. If the supposition that strategy is about creating competitive advantage is accepted, it must also be accepted that some organizations will outperform others. With this in mind, the next question becomes what is it about the strategies of the more successful organizations that are different from the strategies of the less successful organizations? The quest for the answer to this question has been the topic of numerous debates, the subject of several trees worth of journal articles, and has led to the development of some very successful consulting practices. In other words, there are a lot of people with a lot of different opinions as to what makes for successful strategies, and it would be imprudent to even pretend that all of those efforts could be fully explored in this one research project. Nevertheless, it is prudent to review some of the predominant paradigms in the strategy formulation literature, discuss how those ontologies relate to the current research effort, and provide some insight into how those schemas were leveraged.

Strategy efforts can be framed into two sets of activities. The first set encompasses the strategy formulation process. This process typically includes considering alternative courses of action, establishing criteria for selecting among the alternatives, and making comparisons and choices among those alternatives (Hatch, 1997). Once a strategy is formulated it must be implemented. The implementation process typically involves resource allocation, development of control and feedback systems, and creation of structures and policies to support the chosen alternatives (Hatch, 1997). This research, however, is explicitly focused on the strategy formulation process and will not attempt to address implementation activities beyond recognizing their importance.

Strategy could be analogized to singing in that many people think they can do it, only a few people can do it well, and many of those who do not know how to do it well are completely unaware of how inept their skills actually are. It is almost impossible to find a website for even the smallest consulting firm that does not purport to offer some kind of strategic planning services. It takes very little effort, however, to realize that many of the firms who claim to offer these services have extremely creative definitions of what they are labeling as strategy. The degree to which these views deviate from the generally accepted view in the academic and professional literature can very from simple issues of nomenclature to borderline negligence.

Those that do have a firm understanding of strategy, however, often frame those definitions in terms of the development of some kind of plan for future action. Additional context is added to this framing by considering Mintzberg's assertion that strategies should not be thought of as just plans for the future, but also patterns from the past (1987). What he means by this is that while the words on the pages of a strategic plan often use forward looking language like vision, goal, and objectives; the genesis of those plans is rooted in the history and habits of the organization to which they apply. According to Mintzberg, the impact of past histories means that strategies are not only formed by deliberate action, but can also emerge as a result of some evolving situation (1987).

It should also come as no surprise that the goals and objectives of more deliberatively formulated strategies tend to be realized more often than those that just happen to evolve (Hrebinaik & Joyce, 2001; Mintzberg, 1987). There are numerous possible drivers of this reality, not the least of which is the phenomenon that organizations tend to evolve in the direction of where they focus their attention and energies (Cooperrider & Sekerka, 2003). Keeping these facts in mind, it is not a great leap of logic to assume that if an organization is more focused and deliberative about a strategy, they are more likely to be successful. Since deliberative strategy formulation is really an issue of organizational decision making (Hatch, 1997), and organizational decision making is often a function of what mental models the organization is employing (Senge, 1994), the next step in this effort is considering the dominant metal models relevant to strategy formulation.

Strategy as an Organization Responding to Its Environment

Michael Porter is one of the most widely read thinkers on business strategy. His book *Competitive Strategy* is often cited, and his Five-Forces model is considered by many professional managers to be a useful framework for analyzing the different influences that impact the success of their organizations (Argyres & McGahan, 2002; Silbiger, 1999). Just about anyone who has taken even an undergraduate business course is aware of this information. What they may not be as aware of, however, is exactly what Porter's view of strategy really is.

In Porter's own words, "The essence of formulating a competitive strategy is relating a company to its environment" (Porter, 1980). This view was later clarified when Porter said that organizations need to base their strategies on what they can do that is unique compared to their competitors (Porter, 1996). Porter is concerned with how organizations chose to distinguish themselves in the market place. In other words, how do organizations position themselves relative to their competitors and other factors in their environment?

While Porter is by far the most well known advocate of this approach, he is not the only one. Greenwald and Kahn, for example, take the position that organizations can out perform their competitors by being better at supplying their customers than their competitors, creating more demand for their offerings than those of their competitors, or having better economies of scale than their competitors (2005). In other words, they advocate a combative metaphor where the goal is to outmaneuver and defeat the competition. Kim and Mauborgne, on the other hand, advocate that a combative approach is unproductive and recommend understanding where the competitors are, and then going where they are not (2005). This could almost be conceptualized as success by avoiding direct confrontation. While both of these approaches offer newer perspectives; it could be argued that each, and most of the other competition based strategy formulation methods, are simply refinements and derivations of Porter's model rather than unique ways of understanding how strategies are developed and implemented.

While the positionist approach has had some success, there are problems with it. By Porter's own accounts, this tactic focuses on making decisions based primarily on competitors and the environment (Porter, 1996, Porter, 1998; Porter, 2001). While taking these factors into account is important, it creates a situation where organizations are making decisions primarily based on elements that they cannot directly control. Moreover, the pace with which markets and competition change, compared to the time it takes to develop and implement a strategy based upon a solely positionist perspective, actually has some managers thinking that this approach is too slow and too reactive to meet their needs (Collis & Montgomery, 1995). This is in addition to the issue that taking such an approach requires organizations to base critical decisions almost entirely on what their *enemies* are doing. Returning to the previously mentioned war analogy and to the wisdom of Sun Tzu, there is evidence that making movements based solely upon the actions of opponents can be unwise (Griffith, 1963). While it is important to consider this information, an alternative approach might be to start off reviewing the organization's strengths, and then determining how to exploit those advantages in terms of what the competition is doing. While positioning is vital information to consider during strategic analysis, that information alone does not provide enough data to develop a truly sustainable competitive advantage.

Strategy as an Organization Leveraging Core Capabilities

As early as 1992, the Harvard Business Review was publishing articles that identified capabilities as a potential differentiator that enabled organizations such as Wal-Mart and Honda to outperform their rivals (Stalk et al., 1992). One of the main tenets of this view is that success is dependent on transforming an organization's key processes into strategic capabilities that provide superior value to the marketplace. Two of the major champions of this view are Gary Hamel and C.K. Prahalad who advocate that the way an organization should start to think about developing sustainable competitive advantage is by looking inward to what they refer to as core competencies (Hamel & Prahalad, 1994a). Core competencies, according to Hamel and Prahalad, are a bundle of skills and technologies that enable the organization to provide a particular benefit to its customers. Another way to phrase this might be to define core competencies as those differentiating capabilities that make the organization who and what it is. The commitment an organization makes to building core competencies is a commitment to creating or further perfecting its ability to deliver benefits to customers. It is not necessarily a commitment to some specific product or market-opportunity, but to a way of delivering what customers want. Not just what the organization does, but also how it undertakes those activities. As a result, properly developed core competencies can stay consistent, and consistently add value, across product and service categories.

Capabilities have been described in a number of ways, including "the collective skills, abilities, and expertise of an organization" (Ulrich & Smallwood, 2004). The challenge is that developing capabilities that are difficult for competitors to imitate can be costly and time consuming. Organizations must seriously evaluate the strategic value of a particular core competency before deciding to make the development investment (Hamel & Prahalad, 1989). While the book value of the assets developed from these investments may not deteriorate with use and age like physical assets, and in many cases can actually grow with use over time (Prahalad & Hamel, 1990), they do require the organization to consciously devote not only capital but also time to growing them. British Airways is an example of an organization that chose to differentiate itself by offering superior service even though the costs of developing the core competencies associated with that capability ended up being significant (Iacobucci, 1996; Prokesch, 1995; Weiser, 1995). By making the commitment to growing this core competency, however, British Airways has developed a strategic advantage that it is able to maintain, even when the unique aspects of the market evolve and change. To provide sustainable competitive advantage, capabilities and positioning strategies must not only be difficult to imitate, but also adaptable to the evolving environment.

Complicating this issue is the emerging paradigm that it is becoming more and more difficult for organizations to differentiate themselves from their competitors based on product features and benefits alone

(Vandermerwe, 2000). The environment, what positioning is concerned with, may change overnight, such as with the case of the introduction of the internet, or the implosion of the technology bubble. Maintaining the uniqueness of features and benefits, what core competencies contribute to, is also becoming more and more difficult due to the fact that the cycle time during which those benefits can remain unique continues to become shorter and shorter and the barriers for entry of new competitors into some markets are becoming lower. This begs the question of what are best in class organizations doing to differentiate themselves in the marketplace? More and more evidence is pointing to the notion that it is the intangible assets, such as customer relationships, that are starting to make the difference in the performance of organizations, and that the truly successful organizations are the ones that focus their attention on developing and managing those kinds of assets (Hansen & Wernerfelt, 1989; Kaplan & Norton, 2001; Rucci et al., 1998; Vargo & Lusch, 2004).

The Evolving Customer Management Paradigm

Customer management reflects the new direction for business strategies (Kaplan & Norton, 2004). Many organizations claim to focus on their customers, but saying something and doing it are often two very different things. Complicating factors to this issue include the growth of the information economy, and the increasing number of well informed consumers. These paradigms are driving a market that is continually placing more and more demands on organizations and thereby making the management of the intangible assets that impact customer management more and more challenging (Porter, 2001; Urban, 2004; Wilson et al., 2002). The result is that it can become more and more difficult for a company to maintain a leadership position in the market. This assertion is evidenced by the fact that between 1972 and 2002 the likelihood that companies in leadership positions in their particular markets would lose those positions more than doubled (Viguerie & Thompson, 2005). Given the evidence that market leaders are facing such challenges, logic would seem to dictate that other organizations are facing even greater challenges.

Despite these challenges, however, there are several examples of organizations that have been able to not only survive, but also thrive, in the current environment. Harley-Davidson, Southwest Airlines, the Body Shop and Patagonia have all become successful by focusing not just on what they provide to their customers (i.e., the tangibles), but also the approach they use to provide those services (i.e., the intangibles) (Bhattacharya & Sen, 2003; Gittell, 2001). While product quality cannot be ignored, the lack of defects alone will not be a sole differentiator of success. If this were not the case, Harley-Davidson would be no different than Honda or Suzuki, Southwest would be no different than U.S. Air or Delta; the Body Shop would be losing sales to K-Mart's generic products on their cosmetics isle; and Patagonia would be no different from the dozens of other companies that make heavy coats. Building on the earlier assumptions that intangible factors are key differentiators of success, and that strategies provide the framework for how organizations will manage themselves, the question must be asked as to what is it that differentiates these successful organizations' strategy formulation processes from the rest of the market place such that they enable the organizations to effectively address those intangible factors? This question is further complicated by the facts that traditional strategic analysis and decision making tools have tended to look more at financial and capital assets, regardless of whether they take a positionist or capabilities based approach (Luehrman, 1998; Worley et al., 1996).

There are examples in both the popular and academic literature of organizations that are developing strategies to manage these intangible assets effectively. Kaplan and Norton provide an excellent example of how the North American Marketing and Refining (NAM&R) arm of Mobile Oil improved operating cash flow by more than $1 Billion a year in large part by focusing on their customers' needs and finding ways to meet them (2001). Their approach was more aligned with a capabilities based line of thinking advocated by Hamel and Prahalad in that they looked at who their customers were and tried to figure out how to enhance or build competencies to support those customers. Harrah's Casinos used a variety of customer segmentation and analytic techniques to identify who their most valuable customers were and then adjusted the organization's strategy to focus on those customers' needs (Gulati & Oldroyd, 2005; Sutton & Klein, 2003). What they found was that most of their revenue came not from the big spenders that the gaming industry had historically focused on, but from middle income and retiree gamers who were largely ignored by the competition. Harrah's approach was to shift their service and marketing strategies to position themselves to concentrate on this underserved, yet high revenue, segment of the market. By changing their focus to better serving this particular customer segment, Harrah's was able to create substantial growth, even in a weak economy (Loveman, 2003; Sutton & Klein, 2003).

Each organization engaged a different strategy to improve their performance by understanding their customers' unique needs and adjusting accordingly. Both organizations saw great success from their efforts, and continue to grow because of it. The question that is relevant to this research, however, is what do both of these approaches have in common? The answer is that they both focused on customers in general, and how to meet those particular customers' needs. This leads to the conclusion that to be successful; strategies must incorporate not just capabilities and/or position against competitors, but also customers as a distinct unit of analysis. To do that effectively, however, a new model of strategy formulation is needed.

An Eye Towards an Integrated Model

Cummings and Worley define a model as a simplification of an idea for the sake of study and understanding (2005). Senge describes models in terms of assumptions, generalizations, or even pictures that add to understanding and better enable the ability to take action (1994). The model for this research was developed based upon six suppositions that were derived from a review of the available literature:

1. The intent of strategy is to create sustainable competitive advantage that allows organizations to outperform their competitors over time
2. If an organization is more focused and deliberative about how they develop a strategy, they are more likely to be successful
3. While positioning is a vital input during strategic analysis, that information alone does not provide enough perspective to completely develop a truly sustainable competitive advantage
4. Capabilities do contribute to strategic advantage, but that advantage can only be maintained so long as they are difficult for competitors to imitate
5. To maintain competitive advantage, capabilities and positioning strategies must not only be difficult to imitate, but also adaptable to the evolving environment

6. To provide ongoing competitive advantage, strategies must be based not just capabilities and/or position against competitors, but also on customers as a distinct unit of analysis

The first theme that can be derived from these suppositions addresses what ends strategy is meant to achieve, or the outcome that a strategic planning model intends to enable. Those intended ends are the ability to outperform other organizations. Performance is much like art in that it is as much in the eye of the beholder as it is an objective construct. In *Good to Great* for example, performance is defined as terms of stock market returns (Collins, 2001). Johnson, on the other hand, discusses performance in terms of customer loyalty (2002), while Garvin discusses performance in terms of quality as assessed by external metrics such as the Baldridge Award (1991). A newer view on organizational performance contends that performance is not just about measuring how well the organization serves itself, but how much it added to the greater good and the sustainability of the global environment (Hart & Milstein, 1999). Regardless of what criteria are used to define performance, the case can be made that properly developed and applied strategy is a key differentiator in that success.

The second major theme is that strategies that are more deliberatively developed tend to be more successful than those that evolve fortuitously. This is consistent with both the rationalist model view of management theory (Hrebinaik & Joyce, 2001; Mintzberg, 1987), as well as a more social constructionist based view that says that organizations tend to evolve in the direction of where they focus their energy (Cooperrider & Sekerka, 2003). Despite general agreement that the deliberativeness is critical, there does not appear to be a current model that explicitly calls out deliberativeness as a factor in the strategy formulation process. The model that was developed for this research addresses the deficiency.

The third major theme that is apparent from a review of the six suppositions is that an organization should take multiple perspectives into account during the strategy formulation process. This theme is consistent with the call of the likes of Cummings and Angwin who identified the need for a multi-dimensional model of strategy formulation that retains the strengths of previous models while providing managers with additional tools to manage in an ever changing environment (2004). Kaplan and Norton's work on the Balanced Scorecards have been attempts to address this issue (2001; 2004), as has Epstein and Westbrook's Action-Profit Linkage Model (2001), and the Employee-Customer-Profit Chain work that was done at Sears (Rucci et al., 1998). Each of these three models demonstrates the value of a multi-dimensional approach, and acknowledges the need for an organization's efforts to be driven by a well formed strategy. What none of these models do, however, is explicitly define how those strategies should be developed. A review of the strategy literature has reveals that there is a need to more actively integrate the customer perspective into the strategy formulation process as a distinct unit of analysis, and not just as a competing force as defined in Porter's Five Forces model. The rationale for this position is based upon the application of systems theory.

The two sides of systems theory are the view of organizations as open systems that are in active exchange with their environment (French & Bell, 1999), and a systems thinking ontology that focuses on understanding the full patterns of behaviors of the various parts of the organization as an interactive whole (Senge, 1994). Systems thinking is an alternative to the reductionist approach that seeks to break concepts in to smaller and smaller components for sake of understanding, but sometimes fails to link those components back together in a way that creates a full understanding of the organization and the environment in which it operates (Senge, 1994). As such, leveraging an approach like systems theory could be useful in heeding Porter's own caution that organizations must do more than the basic level of analysis if they want to be successful in performing against their competitors (1980).

The goal of a systems theory approach is to understand interrelationships and patterns, rather than just simply snapshots and static single points of data. An approach to strategy formulation that incorporates this ontology could respond to the suppositions of this research that contend that strategy formulation paradigms sometimes focus too much on a single perspective. Taking multiple perspectives into account, the current research explicitly defines the pieces of the organizational system that should be integrated into the strategy formulation process. Based upon the previously identified suppositions; which hold that organizations should take into account their competitors, capabilities, and customers; the model used in this research incorporated that requirement, and also looks at how those different components are integrated into the strategic decision making process.

It has been posited that the management literature relative to strategy spends much more time focusing on how organizations get from *here* to *there*, rather than understanding how they decide where *there* really should be (Gupta, 1980). While the likes of Porter, and Hamel and Prahalad have made progress in addressing this issue by offering different perspectives on the kinds of data should be incorporated into those decisions, the majority of organizations still seem to be making those decisions by what Khatri refers to as intuitive synthesis (1994). This is basically the process where decisions are made based on distilled experience that is gained over time with a process. In other words, it seems to be that experiential judgment is the predominant methodology in strategic decision making. While there does not seem to be much in the traditional business literature about these experiential judgment based approaches other than acknowledging their influence, the few description of these process that can be found appear to be consistent with what scholars who operate from a behavioral sciences based perspective tend to refer as sense-making.

Sense-making is an attempt by individuals in organizations to explain sets of clues from their respective environments, whether internal or external, and use that data to make decisions (Maitlis, 2005). This process is of critical importance since there is evidence of a link between the quality of these sense-making activities and organizational outcomes (Maitlis, 2005; Thomas et al., 1993). There does not, however, appear to be a model of strategic formulation that takes this process explicitly into account (Brown, 2006). Since the goal of this research is to advance the study of strategy formulation, the process of sense-making was added to the model in an effort to understand how organizations synthesize various kinds of data into their strategic decisions.

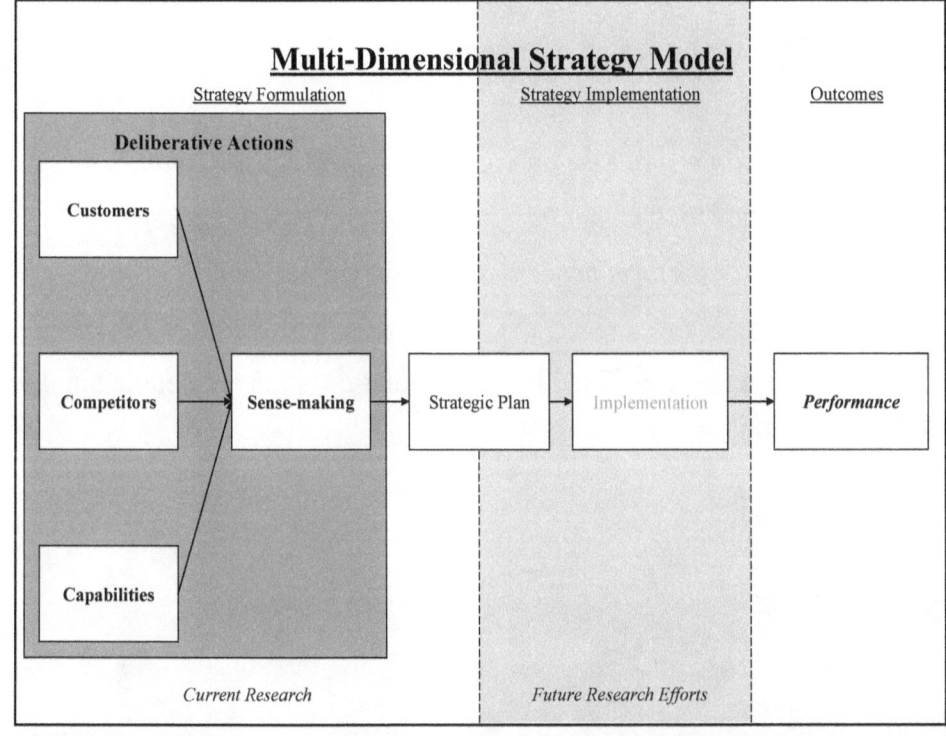

Figure 1. Multi-Dimensional Strategy Model

Figure 1 illustrates the incorporation of the various components that make up the model that was used in this research. Given that the resulting model represents a multi-dimensional perspective on strategy formulation, it will be referred to as the *Multi-Dimensional Strategy Model* or MDSM going forward. Assuming that the suppositions of this research are valid, logic would dictate that the proposed MDSM provides an accurate representation of how organizations can effectively develop their strategies. Just because a conclusion appears logical, however, does not necessarily mean that it is true or even supported by available data (Chalmers, 1999; Kuhn, 1996). To determine if this model is supported by real world data it was tested via the following research question:

Do organizations that take an approach to strategy formulation that is consistent with a model based on a systems thinking perspective perform better than the overall market?

The methods that were used to explore that question are detailed in the next section of this report.

Research Methods

Research Design

A research design is nothing more than a plan for conducting a study in such a way as to answer the research question (Stone, 1978). The first step in developing such a plan is understanding the research question. The research question for this study is

Do organizations that take an approach to strategy formulation that is consistent with a model based on a systems thinking perspective perform better than the overall market?

The effort to explore this research question had two components:

- Do organizations that use to such a model perform better than those that do not?
- What is common across organizations that do use such a model?

The first component lends itself to more empirical research because; depending on how performance is defined; predictive hypotheses can be developed, tested, and then either retained or rejected based upon the resulting data. The second component does not lend itself towards a predictive hypothesis and is therefore classified as *exploratory* in nature (Rudestam & Newton, 2001). Being that this effort has a research question that lends itself to a mix-methodology, it employed what Creswell calls a concurrent nested strategy where both the quantitative and qualitative data are collected together, but the analysis occurs in separate, yet related, phases (2003). This approach is consistent with several other studies related to business strategies and their outcomes (Collins, 2001; Gupta, 1980; Khatri, 1994).

Quantitative Phase

Quantitative research is based upon an epistemological perspective that knowledge is derived from logical inferences and direct observation (Rudestam & Newton, 2001). It tends to be more prescriptive in its approach, and often employs a priori predictions stated in the form of hypotheses (Pophan & Sirotnik, 1992). The research question for this study is about discovering whether organizations that use a model of strategy formulation that is consistent with a systems thinking based perspective perform better than those that do not. Therefore, the independent variable is use of a systems thinking based model, while the dependent variable is performance.

To permit incorporation of this model into a proper experimental design, the variables must be operationally defined so that they can be appropriately measured. Operational definition of a variable means to develop a description of that variable in concrete terms (Grimm, 1993). Being that a model of strategy formulation that is consistent with a systems thinking perspective was developed previously, the operational definition for this research effort was defined as the degree to which an organization uses a strategy formulation process consistent with the *Multi-Dimensional Strategy Model* described in Figure 1.

The next determination was the concrete terms that were employed for performance in this research study. Being that financial performance (e.g., sales, profits, stock performance) has been used in many strategy studies, financial performance was selected as the general category of the performance outcomes for this project. The two specific outcome measures in this study were stock performance over a set period of time, and gross sales. These variables were chosen because they have commonly agreed to definitions over the full spectrum of performance, and this type of data is readily available about publicly traded companies (Collins, 2001).

Performance outcomes related to business strategies are typically lagging measures and the results of the strategy formulation efforts may not be immediately apparent (Kaplan & Norton, 2001; Kaplan & Norton, 2004). Because of this, any effort to study strategy formulation that utilizes a classical experimental design methodology would need to have the flexibility of a longer time horizon to both develop an appropriate sample that can account for potentially moderating variables, as well as allow for the impact of the strategy formulation process on the organizations' performance. Very few examples of strategy formulation studies that meet those strict criteria were located in the literature. One of the limitations of the current study is that it was part of a doctoral dissertation and therefore had a finite amount of time available for completion. This negated the possibility of multiple data collection waves over multiple years, as well as an indefinite measurement period to determine if results were indeed effective. As a result, a classic experimental style study was determined to not be feasible for this effort and an alternative approach was employed.

Numerous examples of strategy related studies were found where questionnaires were distributed to organizations that met some set of predetermined criteria, and those organizations' responses were examined to determine the degree to which they supported the hypotheses of the research question (Harrington et al., 2004; Kirby, 2005; Panayides, 2004; Ramanujam et al., 1986). This approach is consistent with what has been termed a *quasi-experimental* design in that, while it does not meet all the control tests of a classical experimental design, it is still based on a priori predictions in the form of hypotheses and rests upon an epistemological perspective that knowledge is derived from logical inferences and direct observation (Kerlinger & Lee, 2000; Nicholas & Katz, 1985; Pophan & Sirotnik, 1992). This approach was determined to be the best option for this study because it allowed for a maximization of experimental rigor within the available parameters. This approach involved identifying organizations that met the defined performance criteria, and then determining the degree to which those organizations' strategy formulation processes are consistent with the proposed model. This determination was based on the organizations' responses to a questionnaire that was developed based on the previously described Multi-Dimensional Strategy Model (MDSM). Figure 2 illustrates this approach.

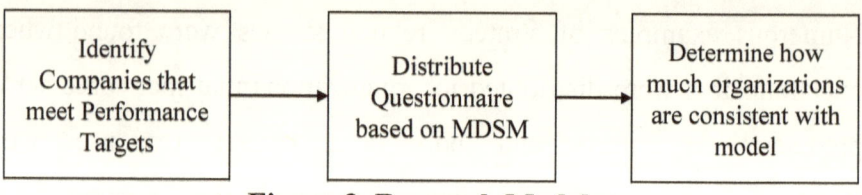

Figure 2. Research Model

The quantitative phase of this study sought to understand the degree to which top performing organizations employed a strategy formulation methodology consistent with the previously described Multi-Dimensional Strategy Model (MDSM). The goal was to determine whether these top performing organizations employ a similar model, and if so whether it was to a degree that could be considered statistically significant. Statistical significance is a matter of determining that something is occurring more often than could be expected by chance alone (Grimm, 1993; Kerlinger & Lee, 2000; Pophan & Sirotnik, 1992). The methods that were used to make those determinations will be described in the Data Analysis & Results section. Those determinations drove decisions to retain or reject hypotheses that were derived from the MDSM. These hypotheses are specifically aligned to particular components of the MDSM. Figure 3 illustrates how the components of the MDSM and each of these hypotheses correspond.

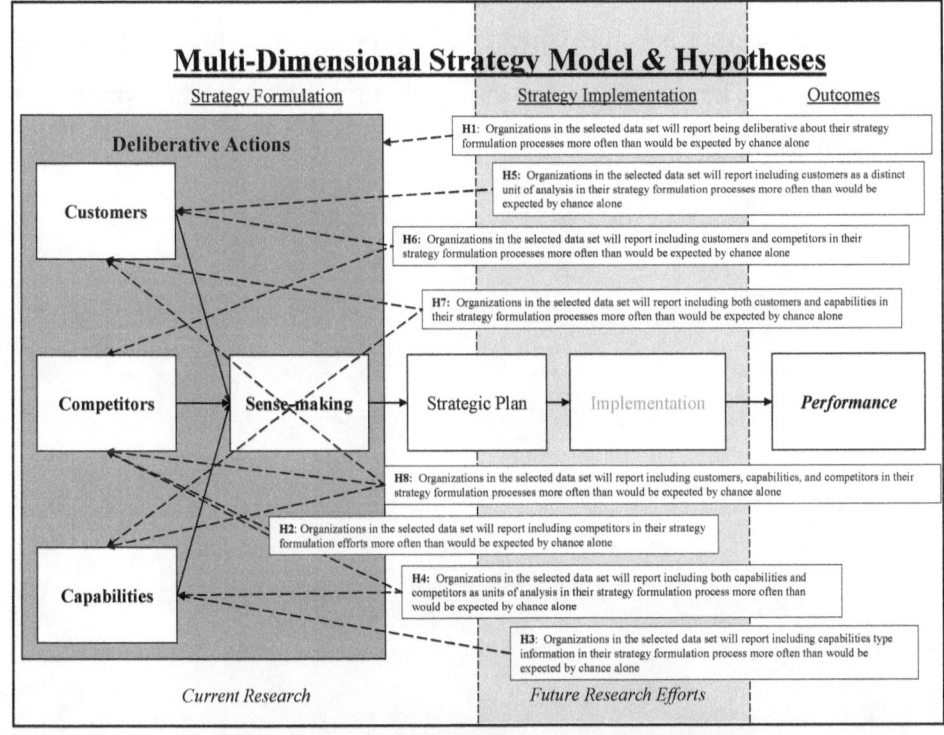

Figure 3. Hypotheses Alignment to MDSM

Of particular note is that no hypotheses correspond to the sense-making component of the MDSM. As previously discussed, sense-making type activities have been one of the least explored areas of strategy formulation. This may be due to sense-making being more of a process of social construction where individuals attempt to interpret and explain the data they see in their environment (Maitlis, 2005), and sense-making having a more interpretivist nature (Giola et al., 1994). This interpretivist nature makes the concept difficult to operationally define, and as such ill-suited for quantitative research, which has been a major part of most strategy related studies to date. What sense-making is better suited for, however, is qualitative research that seeks to understand commonalities across various aspects of a set of activities so that a better conceptualization of these processes can be developed. The approach for the qualitative phase of this project is described in the following section.

Qualitative Phase

Typically, qualitative methods do not intend to test or prove some particular concept, so much as explore a phenomena further and gain greater insights (Creswell, 2003; Rudestam & Newton, 2001). The objective of the qualitative phase of this study was to identify commonalities across the processes used by the participating organizations so that further details could be incorporated into the MDSM. The intent of doing so would be to achieve a better understanding of the kinds of data that are used in those processes relative to competitors, capabilities, and customers. In addition, the qualitative data relative to those constructs, as well as the data relative to sense-making, would be analyzed via appropriate qualitative methods. This is because sense-making is a critical management activity that involves the interpretation of key events (Maitlis, 2005). The assumption was that some kind of sense-making does occur, regardless of whether the people involved in the process realize that is what they are doing or not.

Since qualitative research does not rely on a priori hypotheses, it must instead be guided by what will be termed here as questions of inquiry. In particular, this effort is looking to engage in modified narrative research that seeks to understand the feedback of study participants. This narrative research is guided by the following four questions. The alignment of these questions to the MDSM is illustrated in Figure 4.

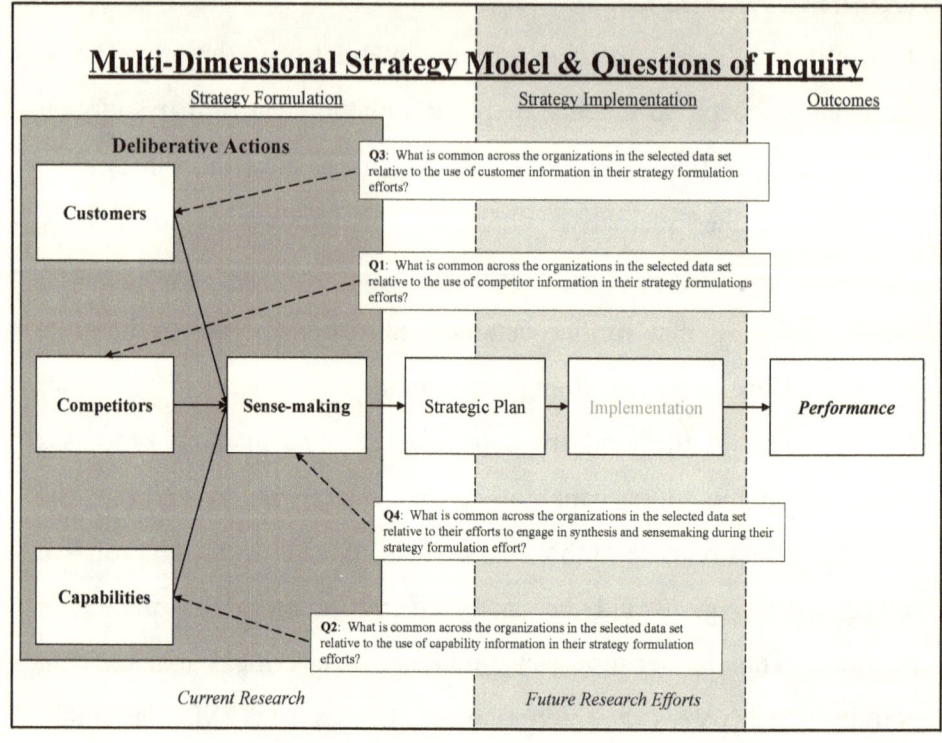

Figure 4. MDMS and Questions of Inquiry

Given that this study is employing a concurrent nested strategy where both the quantitative and qualitative data are collected during the same process, the items used to collect this data were incorporated into the same questionnaire that was used to collect data for the quantitative phase of this project. The process for developing this questionnaire is described in the next section.

Questionnaire Development

Two common ways of developing data collection questionnaires are by either beginning with an existing questionnaire and then modifying it to meet the needs of the current study (Harrington et al., 2004; Watson & Wooldridge, 2005), or creating an entirely new questionnaire based on the domain being studied (Panayides, 2004). The advantage of starting with an existing questionnaire is that it allows for increased transparency as to how the items were developed, while the advantage of developing a custom questionnnaire is increased applicability to the concept being studied. The challenges appear to be that using an existing questionnaire may not fully meet the needs of the research effort, while using a custom questionnaire may require more development effort and may be more easily challenged if the process for developing that questionnaire is not fully documented. Being that this study is centered on the MDSM and there has never been a previous study using that model, beginning with an existing data collection tool would not be appropriate. As such a custom questionnaire was developed.

Stone recommends a process referred to as mapping to understand how items within some domain correspond to a set of items in a measurement tool (1978). Earlier, the various quantitative hypotheses and qualitative questions of inquiry were graphically mapped to the various components of the MDSM, as illustrated in Figure 3 and Figure 4. The deliberative action component maps to H_1. The competition component maps to H_2, H_4, H_6, H_8, and Q_1. The capabilities component maps to H_3, H_4, H_7, H_8 and Q_2. The customers component maps to H_5, H_6, H_7, H_8 and Q_3. The sense-making component maps to Q_4.

Based upon these mappings, five sets of questions were required to gather the information necessary to determine whether the organizations in the selected group employ strategy formulation processes consistent with the MDSM. In addition, a set of information-based questions was required to support appropriate demographic and non-response bias analysis. A question to determine the degree to which those organizations perceive their strategy efforts as impacting their performance was also included since that issue is directly related to one of the main criticisms of the existing paradigms (Collis & Montgomery, 1995). As a result, there were seven question sets in the data collection questionnaire. These sections are described below.

- Section 1 – Identification Items: These items are used to determine which organization was reporting the data. This includes questionnaire items 1 – 6
- Section 2 – Strategy Impact Items: This section addresses the concerns of researchers who report that business strategies are not perceived as impactful on organizational performance. This section includes one five-point Likert scale item asking respondents to rate the perceived impactfulness of their strategy development efforts, and one open-ended item asking

the respondents to describe the kinds of criteria that it uses to classify itself as performing well, or not performing well. This section includes questionnaire items 7 and 8

- Section 3 – Deliberativeness of the Strategy Process: This section includes one five-point Likert scale item asking the respondents to rate how deliberative its strategy formulation efforts are, as well as an open ended item asking the respondents to describe the process it uses. This section includes questionnaire items 9 and 10, and is associated with H_1

- Section 4 – Use of Competitive Information: This section includes one five-point Likert scale item asking respondents to rate the degree to which they include information about competition and the environment in their strategy formulation processes, and an open ended item asking them to describe the data elements they include in those efforts. This section includes questionnaire items 11 and 12; and is associated with H_2, H_4, H_6, H_8 and Q_1

- Section 5 – Use of Capabilities Information: This section includes one five-point Likert scale item asking respondents to rate the degree to which they include information about capabilities in their strategy formulation processes, and an open ended item asking them to describe what data elements they include in those efforts. This section includes questionnaire items 13 and 14; and is associated with H_3, H_4, H_7, H_8 and Q_2

- Section 6 – Use of Customer Information: This section includes one five-point Likert scale item asking respondents to rate the degree to which they include information about customers and their needs in the organizations strategy formulation processes, and an open ended item asking the respondents to describe what data elements they include in those efforts. This section includes questionnaire items 15 and 16; and is associated with H_5, H_6, H_7, H_8 and Q_3

- Section 7 – Sense-making: This section includes one open ended item that asks respondent to describe the processes they use to understand and utilize the various kinds of data during their organizations' strategy formulation processes. This section includes questionnaire item 17 and is associated with Q_4

The decision was made to administer this questionnaire via the internet as this methodology has the advantage of being easy to administer, allows for fast and immediate processing of data, and is in alignment with a cutting-edge mentality (Church & Waclawski, 1998). The primary criticism of this methodology is that it requires respondents to have access to a computer terminal, some degree of computer literacy, and network connectivity (Church & Waclawski, 1998). These criticisms, however, were not expected to be an issue for this research given that the use of computers and the internet has become largely ubiquitous in today's business environment. The data collection tool was developed using the ZipSurvey application (www.zipsurvey.com), with each section having its own page as part of the on-line questionnaire.

Participant Selection

The process for identifying organizations to use in a study can take many forms. Organizations may be randomly sampled, or they may be purposefully selected. The goal of sampling is to take some cross-section of the population that is representative of that entire universe so as to reduce the likelihood that the feedback from the respondents is markedly different that the population as a whole (Kerlinger & Lee, 2000). This is in contrast to the purposeful selection approach that seeks out individuals or organizations that meet very specific criteria related to the topic of the research study. A key point of differentiation is that the sampling approach assumes that the results from the study can be assumed to apply to an entire population. A purposeful selection makes no such assumptions and recognizes that the results are only necessarily applicable to those entities that were part of that particular study. While some researchers may question the reliability of this approach, if a group of entities are selected based on some unique characteristic that differentiates them from the broader population, and the goal of the study is related to that characteristic, then a purposeful selection approach is appropriate. This is not unlike the case study approaches employed in a great many management research efforts, examples of which can be found not only in *Good to Great* and *Built to Last* (Collins, 2001; Collins & Porras, 2002), but also in the numerous texts on topics like the Balanced Scorecard (Kaplan & Norton, 2001; Kaplan & Norton, 2004). Being that there are numerous examples of purposeful selection being used in management research, this methodology was employed for this study.

What must now be better understood is how these organizations were selected.

Purposeful selection can take either quantitative or qualitative approaches. Collins employed a more quantitative approach when selecting companies to study in *Good to Great* by identifying organizations that had a total stock return of at least three times the general market from a point of transition through the fifteen subsequent years (2001). One of the more prominent examples of a qualitative approach was when Tom Peters identified companies to study for *In Search of Excellence* by asking the partners at McKinsey and Company who they thought was a "cool" organization (2001). Since the decision has already been made to use financial performance measures as the primary outcome variables in this effort, a quantitative approach was determined to be the most appropriate option.

As previously stated, the benefits of using financial measures are that they have agreed upon definitions of performance, and that this information is easy to obtain in the case of publicly traded organizations. This availability of data is due in large part to the reporting requirement of the Securities and Exchange Commission. Numerous avenues were available for obtaining this data, and the decision that needed to be made was determining the best options for identifying top performers in terms of stock price and gross sales. In terms of stock price, the decision was made to purchase a data-set from the Center for Research in Security Prices (CRSP) at the

University of Chicago because it maintains several databases that track security prices across multiple markets (2006). The data-set identified and ranked the top 200 performing publicly traded companies in terms of total stock market returns between January 1, 2001 and December 31, 2005. This time period was chosen both because it was the most recent full five year period, and because it was a period of relatively low overall returns relative to the previous five year period. The reason for selecting this five year period to control for potentially moderating variables such as the stock market bubble that had occurred during the previous five year period. The data-set included the name of each company, their total return ranking, stock trading symbol, and Standard Industry Classification (SIC) code. Additional information was also readily available on various websites such as the *Wall Street Journal* (www.wsj.com) and *Fortune Magazine* (www.fortune.com).

In identifying organizations based on gross sales during the previous fiscal year, numerous options were considered but the decision was made to use organizations that were included in the most recent Fortune 500 ranking of top companies in terms of gross sales. This decision was based upon the list being easily obtainable from the www.fortune.com website, and wide recognition that this list includes leading companies. The website lists company name, stock trading symbol, gross sales and profits from the previous year. The list used for this study included sales through December 31, 2005. An additional reason for choosing the Fortune 500 was that lists of names and e-mail addresses for executives in Fortune 500 companies can be easily purchased from several different sources; thereby making the acquisition of contact information relatively manageable. Purchasing names and contact information is consistent with several other studies that were reviewed as a part of this project (Panayides, 2004; Ramanujam et al., 1986; Watson & Wooldridge, 2005).

Data Collection

It is axiomatic that quality data makes for quality studies. The goal of the data collection methodology for this study was to drive a response rate that would be as high as possible so that the level of confidence in the findings could be maximized. The data collection phase of this study had two sub-phases. The first sub-phase focused on efforts to collect data from organizations that were identified by the CRSP as part of the Top 200 performing organizations between 2001 and 2005. Hereafter these organizations will be collectively referred to as the Top 200. The second sub-phase of the data collection focused on collecting data from organizations that were part of the Fortune 500 for 2005. Organizations in this group will hereafter be collectively referred to as the Fortune 500.

One of the challenges with collecting data from the Top 200 was that many of these organizations are relatively small and purchasing contact names and e-mail addresses, as was done with the Fortune 500, was not feasible. Moreover, publicly available information from sources such as WSJ.com and Fortune.com often only listed investor relations contact information; rather than e-mail addresses of individuals who might be involved in the strategy formulation process. What was listed in many cases, however, were general telephone numbers and the names of officers within the organization (referred to as *Insiders* on WSJ.com). Armed with these insights the decision was made to *cold-call* the Top 200 organizations and request to speak with either an individual with a title related to strategy formulation, or someone within the office of the Chief Financial Officer (CFO). The reason for this approach is that while the Chief Executive Officer (CEO) sets the vision for an organization, it is often other senior officers within the firm who have responsibility for doing the actual analysis and planning to figure out how to make those visions a reality (Khatri, 1994). Baring a position such as Vice President of Strategy, those responsibilities often fall to the CFO. Based on this insight, the default approach was to request the CFO, unless another individual with *Strategy* in their title could be readily identified.

As individuals were identified and contacted, anyone who agreed to participate was forwarded an e-mail that provided more details about the study and a link to the on-line questionnaire. In keeping with Panayides' recommendation, reminders were sent to individuals who indicated that they would participate, but who did not respond to the initial e-mail (2004). These reminders were sent approximately two weeks and four weeks after the initial e-mail requests. Of the Top 200 organizations, 91 agreed to receive e-mail requests, 21 declined to participate, and 38 were determined to be not reachable. A total of 48 responses were received from this group, however, only 43 were determined to be usable. Usability determinations were based upon the respondent completing all Likert Scale based items on the questionnaire. Taking this information into account, the final usable response rate for the Top 200 sub-phase of the data collection effort was 26.5%.

Being that names and e-mails for key individuals in Fortune 500 organizations could be purchased from third-party sources, the Fortune 500 sub-phase did not involve any *cold-calling*. The purchased list, however, was reviewed to eliminate contact information for any organization that was not publicly traded, and to then remove contact information for any individual that appeared to be inappropriate for this study (e.g., VP of Accounting). Also, organizations for which contact information was not included in the purchased list were classified as unreachable. The resulting list included contact information for 472 organizations, four of which were also part of the Top 200. Those four companies were not resolicited. As a result, e-mail requests to participate in the study with a hyperlink to the questionnaire were sent to contacts in 468 companies. The e-mails also included the offer of a complementary summary report of the findings of the study if they provided a response. Reminders were forwarded at two and four week intervals after the initial e-mail request.

After each round, e-mails that were returned as undeliverable were reviewed to determine which organizations should be classified as unreachable. A total of 171 organizations listed as part of the Fortune 500 were classified as unreachable during this study. Thirty organizations provided responses to the questionnaire, of which 23 were determined to be usable according criteria consistent with that employed for the responses from the Top 200 organizations. Taking this information into account, the final usable response rate for the Fortune 500 sub-phase of the data collection effort was 7.7%.

Combining the two sub-phases, the overall usable response rate for this effort was 14.4%. Table 1 details this information.

Table 1. Data Collection Response Rates

	Top 200	Fortune 500
Total Population	200	500
Not Publicly Traded	N/A	28
Duplicates from Top 200	N/A	4
Not-Reachable	<u>38</u>	<u>171</u>
Usable Sample	162	297
Total Responses	48	30
Usable Responses	43	23
Response Rate	26.5%	7.7%
Overall Response Rate		14.4%

With the data collected and compiled, the question must now be asked as to what the data says and what new insights can be gained. The next section of this report describes the data analysis efforts and associated outcomes. In particular, these efforts sought to understand if the available data supported the previously stated hypotheses. If the data did show support for those hypotheses, was that support significant enough to rule out the possibility of other influences driving those results. In addition, the effort sought to understand whether anything else could be learned about the strategy formulation process of participating organizations based on the *stories* they told in the open-ended section of the data collection questionnaire.

Data Analysis & Results

Sample Representativeness

Following the advice of Kerlinger and Lee, the first task during the data analysis phase was determining the representativeness of the organizations that agreed to participate in the study verses the total population (2000). One way to undertake such an assessment is to look at the response rate for a study and determine whether it was high enough to be confident that the responses were representative. As previously discussed, the response rates for strategy related studies published in peer reviewed journals were somewhere between 14% - 34% (Harrington et al., 2004; Panayides, 2004; Ramanujam et al., 1986; Watson & Wooldridge, 2005). While the 14.4% response rate for this study is on the low end of that continuum, it is nevertheless within that range. Based upon this determination, and the assumption that publication in peer reviewed journals does require a high degree of academic rigor, the conclusion can be drawn that the response rate for this study is high enough to conclude that the feedback from the participating organizations is at least as representative of the total population as the feedback of respondents in other published strategy focused studies. Based upon this, the data for this study does pass the response rate test for representativeness.

A second way to assess representativeness is to examine the degree to which the demographic characteristics of the respondents mirror the total population (Kerlinger & Lee, 2000). The two demographics that were used for this study were number of employees and total sales volume for 2005. These two demographics were chosen because they were common to all participating organizations, and because this information was readily available from WSJ.com. In both cases, the actual numbers were input into the same MS Access database that was used to track information related to the data collection effort, and then categorized. Table 2 depicts the categorizations of the employee and sales data for both the total population and the responding population. It also identifies the percentage of each group that fell into each category. Table 2 also illustrates the differences between the total and responding populations on a category by category basis.

Table 2. Overall Demographic Comparisons

Total Employees

Total			Responded			
Count	Employees	Percent	Count	Employees	Percent	Diff.
247	> 10000	53.81%	22	> 10000	29.73%	24.08%
47	5000 – 9999	10.24%	7	5000 – 9999	9.46%	0.78%
68	1000 – 4999	14.81%	17	1000 – 4999	22.97%	-8.16%
26	500 – 999	5.66%	8	500 – 999	10.81%	-5.15%
31	250 – 499	6.75%	8	250 – 499	10.81%	-4.06%
22	100 – 250	4.79%	8	100 – 250	10.81%	-6.02%
18	< 100	3.92%	4	< 100	5.41%	-1.48%
459			74			7.10%

Sales for 2005

Total			Responded			
Count	Sales	Percent	Count	Sales	Percent	Diff.
46	> $25B	10.02%	5	> $25B	6.76%	3.27%
94	$10B - $25B	20.48%	7	$10B - $25B	9.46%	11.02%
185	$1B - $10B	40.31%	29	$1B - $10B	39.19%	1.12%
21	$500MM - $1B	4.58%	2	$500MM - $1B	2.70%	1.87%
28	$250MM - $499MM	6.10%	10	$250MM - $499MM	13.51%	-7.41%
41	$100M - $250M	8.93%	9	$100M - $250M	12.16%	-3.23%
22	$50M - $100M	4.79%	6	$50M - $100M	8.11%	-3.32%
22	< $50M	4.79%	6	< $50M	8.11%	-3.32%
459			74			4.32%

While there were some instances where the differences between the total population and the responding population were high enough to warrant caution, the average differences between the total and responding populations for total employees and sales for 2005 were only 7.1% and 4.32% respectively. Those two numbers are small enough to suggest that the organizations that agreed to participate are representative of the total population. To make sure that this is the case, however, a deeper review, based on the two separate populations, is warranted.

The differences in the demographic breakdowns between the total populations and the responding organizations seem to be highest among organizations with larger employee populations and higher gross sales for 2005. This is most likely due to the response rate for the Top 200 organizations, which tend to be smaller and have lower sales volumes, being higher than the response rate for the Fortune 500 organizations. This variation is attributable to the differences in the data collection approaches for the two populations. Each organization in the Top 200 who received an e-mail had verbally committed to participating before being sent the request. By contrast, organizations in the Fortune 500 were not *cold-called* and as such did not make the same commitment before receiving the e-mail requests. Recognizing the potential impact of these different approaches, it is prudent to review the demographic breakdowns of each group separately to determine if the responding organizations appeared to be more similar when viewed in this light. Table 3 and Table 4 detail these comparisons.

Table 3. Top 200 Organizations Demographic Comparison

Total Employees

	Total Population				Responded		
Count	Employees	Percent	Count	Employees		Percent	Diff.
10	> 10000	6.17%	1	> 10000		2.17%	4.00%
10	5000 – 9999	6.17%	5	5000 – 9999		10.87%	-4.70%
47	1000 – 4999	29.01%	12	1000 – 4999		26.09%	2.93%
24	500 – 999	14.81%	8	500 – 999		17.39%	-2.58%
31	250 – 499	19.14%	8	250 – 499		17.39%	1.74%
22	100 – 250	13.58%	8	100 – 250		17.39%	-3.81%
18	< 100	11.11%	4	< 100		8.70%	2.42%
162			46				3.17%

Sales for 2005

	Total Population				Responded		
Count	Sales	Percent	Count	Sales		Percent	Diff.
28	1B – 10B	17.28%	13	1B – 10B		28.26%	-10.98%
21	500MM - 1B	12.96%	2	500MM - 1B		4.35%	8.62%
28	250MM – 499MM	17.28%	10	250MM - 499MM		21.74%	-4.46%
41	100M - 250M	25.31%	9	100M – 250M		19.57%	5.74%
22	50M - 100M	13.58%	6	50M - 100M		13.04%	0.54%
22	< 50M	13.58%	6	< 50M		13.04%	0.54%
162			46				5.14%

Table 4. Fortune 500 Organizations Demographic Comparison

Total Employees

	Total Population			Responded		
Count	Employees	Percent	Count	Employees	Percent	Diff.
237	> 10000	79.80%	21	> 10000	75.00%	4.80%
37	5000 – 9999	12.46%	5	5000 – 9999	17.86%	-5.40%
21	1000 – 4999	7.07%	2	1000 – 4999	7.14%	-0.07%
2	500 – 999	0.67%	0	500 – 999	0.00%	0.67%
0	250 – 499	0.00%	0	250 – 499	0.00%	0.00%
0	100 – 250	0.00%	0	100 – 250	0.00%	0.00%
0	< 100	0.00%	0	< 100	0.00%	0.00%
297			28			2.74%

Sales for 2005

	Total Population			Responded		
Count	Sales	Percent	Count	Sales	Percent	Diff.
46	> 25B	15.49%	5	> 25B	17.86%	-2.37%
94	10B - 25B	31.65%	7	10B – 25B	25.00%	6.65%
157	1B – 10B	52.86%	16	1B – 10B	57.14%	-4.28%
0	500MM - 1B	0.00%	0	500MM - 1B	0.00%	0.00%
0	250MM – 499MM	0.00%	0	250MM – 499MM	0.00%	0.00%
0	100M – 250M	0.00%	0	100M – 250M	0.00%	0.00%
0	50M - 100M	0.00%	0	50M - 100M	0.00%	0.00%
0	< 50M	0.00%	0	< 50M	0.00%	0.00%
297			28			4.43%

Based upon the average differences in the demographic breakdowns in these groups being somewhere between 2.74% and 5.14%, it can be inferred that the demographic makeup of the responding organizations is not markedly different from the overall population. Based upon this insight, the remainder of the research proceeded under the assumption that the sample of responding organizations was sufficiently representative of the total population to pass the hurdle of academic rigor.

Quantitative Analysis & Results

After determining that the results are likely representative, the next step was determining the degree to which the data supports the stated hypotheses (Pophan & Sirotnik, 1992; Rudestam & Newton, 2001). The first determination of support was made based on the directionality of the results, while the second determination of support is based on an assessment of the likelihood that those results were more pronounced than could be expected by chance alone. To begin this effort, the data from the ZipSurvey.com questionnaire was exported to an MS Excel file that was then uploaded to an MS Access database that was also used to track responses during the data collection effort. Using each organization's stock symbol as the key field, the appropriate data was combined into one master table that contained all the appropriate demographic information as well as each organization's responses. This data was re-exported into an MS Excel format that was then uploaded to SPSS.

As described earlier, there were eight hypotheses associated with this study. Four of those hypotheses (H1, H2, H3 and H5) make predictions that can be assessed based on responses to individual questionnaire items. Each of those items was associated with a particular variable within the SPSS database. The four remaining hypotheses (H4, H6, H7 and H8) make predictions about the responding organizations that cannot be assessed from the responses to individual questionnaire items. For those four hypotheses, new variables were created using the SPSS's Compute functionality. These new variables were averages of the scores for the items associated with Competitors, Capabilities and Customers so as to determine the degree to which organizations incorporated more than one view into their strategy formulation activities. Table 5 illustrates the linkage of these hypotheses to the variables in the dataset.

Table 5. Data to Hypothesis linkage

Variable	Formula	Hypothesis
Impact	N/A	N/A – Question included to assess participants perception of strategy's impact on their organization's performance
Deliberative	N/A	H1: Organizations in the selected data-set will report being deliberative about their strategy formulation processes more often than would be expected by chance alone
Competition	N/A	H2: Organizations in the selected data-set will report including competitors in their strategy formulation efforts more often than would be expected by chance alone
Capabilities	N/A	H3: Organizations in the selected data-set will report including core competency type information in their strategy formulation process more often than would be expected by chance alone
Customers	N/A	H5: Organizations in the selected data-set will report including customers as a distinct unit of analysis in their strategy formulation processes more often than would be expected by chance alone
Comp_Cap	= (Competition + Capabilities)/2	H4: Organizations in the selected data-set will report including both capabilities and competitors as units of analysis in their strategy formulation process more often than would be expected by chance alone
Comp_Cust	=(Competition + Customers)/2	H6: Organizations in the selected data-set will report including customers and competitors in their strategy formulation processes more often than would be expected by chance alone
Cap_Cust	=(Capabilities + Customers)/2	H7: Organizations in the selected data-set will report including both customers and capabilities in their strategy formulation processes more often than would be expected by chance alone
Comp_Cap_Cust	=(Competition + Capabilities + Customers)/3	H8: Organizations in the selected data-set will report including customers, capabilities, and competitors in their strategy formulation processes more often than would be expected by chance alone

Once the data manipulation was complete, it was then possible to begin performing appropriate analyses on the data to determine what insights could be gained. The first type of analyses was simple histograms for each of the five variables that were associated with a single item within the questionnaire. Figures 5 illustrate these results.

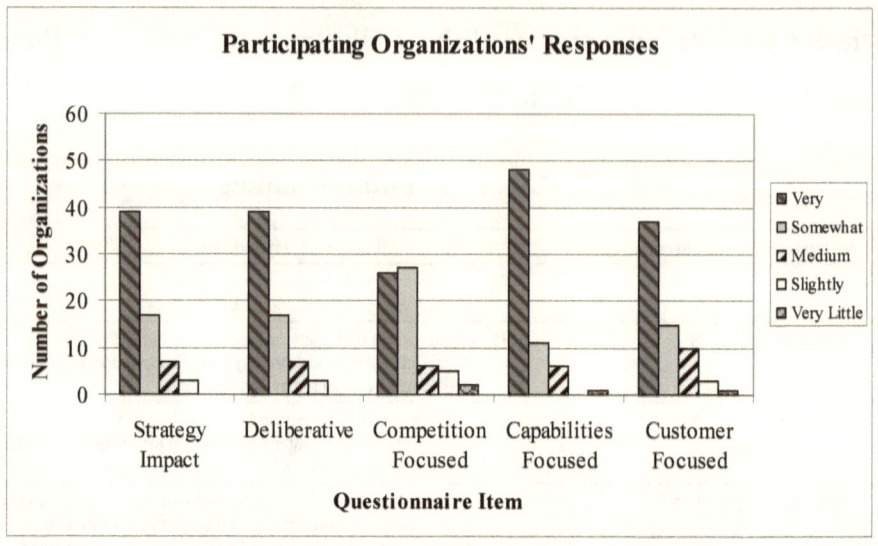

Figure 5. Questionnaire Response Histogram

Clearly the responses to the questionnaire trend towards the positive side of the response scales for each item. This trending is made even more apparent when the means and standard deviations for all items are examined as they are in Table 6. With no single mean below 4.06, the assertion can be made that the positive trend in the data does tend to support the hypotheses that have been presented here. Before a final determination can be made to retain or reject those hypotheses, however, the degree to which these trends are significant must be assessed. This is simply a question of if the observed results are a significant departure from what might be expected by chance alone (Pophan & Sirotnik, 1992). The assumption being that if chance alone can be ruled out, then the expectation is that a real effect is in place.

Table 6. Means and Standard Deviations

Variable	Hypothesis	Mean	Std.	N
Impact	N/A – Question included to assess participants perception of strategy's impact on their organization's performance	4.39	0.86	66
Deliberative	H1: Organizations in the selected data-set will report being deliberative about their strategy formulation processes more often than would be expected by chance alone	4.06	1.15	66
Competition	H2: Organizations in the selected data-set will report including competitors in their strategy formulation efforts more often than would be expected by chance alone	4.06	1.04	66
Capabilities	H3: Organizations in the selected data-set will report including core competency type information in their strategy formulation process more often than would be expected by chance alone	4.59	0.78	66
Customers	H5: Organizations in the selected data-set will report including customers as a distinct unit of analysis in their strategy formulation processes more often than would be expected by chance alone	4.27	0.99	66
Comp_Cap	H4: Organizations in the selected data-set will report including both capabilities and competitors as units of analysis in their strategy formulation process more often than would be expected by chance alone	4.33	0.65	66
Comp_Cust	H6: Organizations in the selected data-set will report including customers and competitors in their strategy formulation processes more often than would be expected by chance alone	4.17	0.79	66
Cap_Cust	H7: Organizations in the selected data-set will report including both customers and capabilities in their strategy formulation processes more often than would be expected by chance alone	4.43	0.76	66
Comp_Cap_Cust	H8: Organizations in the selected data-set will report including customers, capabilities, and competitors in their strategy formulation processes more often than would be expected by chance alone	4.31	0.65	66

While there are numerous statistical techniques available, the decision was made to use the Chi-squared (X^2) test due to its ability to assess the significance between expected and observed frequencies in a given distribution (Pophan & Sirotnik, 1992). The larger the resulting X^2 for each difference, the greater the likelihood that the observed distribution is due to something other than chance (Kerlinger & Lee, 2000). For this study, the X^2 function in SPSS was used to perform these calculations with the expectation that chance alone would result in relatively even distribution of responses across each of the variables.

Table 7 displays each variable, its associated hypothesis, the resulting X^2, the Degrees of Freedom (df) for each variable, as well as the statistical significance of the resulting X^2 calculation. In simplest terms, Degrees of Freedom is an assessment of the number of possible variation within a given item (Pophan & Sirotnik, 1992). When performing a X^2 calculation the df is determined by the number of possible responses to an item minus one. Since each item in the questionnaire for this study used a five point Likert scale, the df for each item is equal to four. For items with df=4, a X^2 equal to or greater than 18.465 would be considered significant at the .001 level. This would mean that such a distribution would be expected less than 0.1% of the time by chance alone. Each of the eight items attached to a hypothesis had a resulting X^2 calculation of at least 32.04 meaning that they were all greater than the necessary threshold for retaining them at the .01 level which is the higher level of rigor normally found in academic research. Based on this, all the hypotheses presented earlier were retained and the conclusion could be drawn that the MDSM does indeed align with the strategy formulation practices of top performing organizations.

Table 7. Chi – Squared Calculations

Variable	Hypothesis	X^2	df	Sig.
Impact	N/A – Question included to assess participants perception of strategy's impact on their organization's performance	54.47	4	0.000
Deliberative	H1: Organizations in the selected data-set will report being deliberative about their strategy formulation processes more often than would be expected by chance alone	32.04	4	0.000
Competition	H2: Organizations in the selected data-set will report including competitors in their strategy formulation efforts more often than would be expected by chance alone	38.84	4	0.000
Capabilities	H3: Organizations in the selected data-set will report including core competency type information in their strategy formulation process more often than would be expected by chance alone	82.30	4	0.000
Customers	H5: Organizations in the selected data-set will report including customers as a distinct unit of analysis in their strategy formulation processes more often than would be expected by chance alone	52.63	4	0.000
Comp_Cap	H4: Organizations in the selected data-set will report including both capabilities and competitors as units of analysis in their strategy formulation process more often than would be expected by chance alone	73.77	4	0.000
Comp_Cust	H6: Organizations in the selected data-set will report including customers and competitors in their strategy formulation processes more often than would be expected by chance alone	74.58	4	0.000
Cap_Cust	H7: Organizations in the selected data-set will report including both customers and capabilities in their strategy formulation processes more often than would be expected by chance alone	54.41	4	0.000
Comp_Cap_Cust	H8: Organizations in the selected data-set will report including customers, capabilities, and competitors in their strategy formulation processes more often than would be expected by chance alone	85.78	4	0.000

While the frequency histogram and X^2 calculations show that the MDSM does reflect the reality of the organizations who participated in this research, they do not directly address the question of whether or not such a model would help drive an organization's performance. While this study has attempted to control for that variable by only including organizations that pass one of two high performance criteria, there has been research showing that strategy formulation processes may not always be a direct driver of an organization's performance

(Dean & Sharfman, 1996). For this reason, an item was included in the questionnaire that specifically inquired as to how impactful the strategy formulation process was on the performance of the participating organizations. As presented in Figure 6, the response pattern does suggest that organizations that participated in this study believe that their strategy formulation efforts have a positive impact on an organization's performance. Table 7 shows that this pattern is associated with a X^2 calculation of 54.473, well above the 18.465 minimum for significance at the .01 level, meaning that there is a very small chance that such a pattern could result by chance alone. This suggests that not only does the proposed MDSM represent reality in terms of the strategic planning processes of high performing organizations, but that those organizations see their strategic planning efforts as having a significant impact on their performance.

Now that the MDSM has been shown to represent reality, and there is evidence suggesting that that reality does positively impact an organization's performance; the question that must now be asked is what is common amongst those processes beyond just focusing on competition, capabilities and competitors? Further, what approaches are organizations using to synthesize and make sense of these disparate kinds of data so that they can be used to make the right business decisions? These questions were explored in the qualitative analysis and results phase of this study.

Qualitative Analysis & Results

Since the hypotheses were retained the focus of the qualitative analysis phase was gaining a deeper understanding of what is common across the strategy formulation processes of the responding organizations so that these insights can be used to add depth to the proposed model. This approach is consistent with the general focus of most qualitative research in that it is not seeking to prove or disprove anything in particular, but is instead seeking to gain greater insights into some particular phenomena (Rudestam & Newton, 2001; Strauss & Corbin, 1998). To develop these understandings, the qualitative phase of research is guided by four previously stated questions of inquiry:

Q_1: What is common across the organizations in the selected data-set relative to the use of competitor information in their strategy formulations efforts?

Q_2: What is common across the organizations in the selected data-set relative to the use of capability information in their strategy formulation efforts?

Q_3: What is common across the organizations in the selected data-set relative to the use of customer information in their strategy formulation efforts?

Q_4: What is common across the organizations in the selected data-set relative to their efforts to engage in synthesis and sense-making during their strategy formulation effort?

The first step in this revised analysis approach was to assimilate the content relevant to each of the four questions of inquiry. To facilitate this process, a combined MS Word document was extracted from the MS Access database, uploaded to Atlas.ti, and subjected to what could best be described as a *macro-coding*. The *macro-coding* effort involved reviewing each section of text and then using Atlas.ti's coding tool to assign labels to sections of text based upon their relevance to the incorporation of customers, capabilities, or competition into the strategy formulation process, or the degree to which the comments described how the organizations attempted to make sense of relevant data sources. Using Atlas.ti's Code Manager function, it was possible to extract all the quotations associated with each of the four questions of inquiry and then create one MS Word file for each question of inquiry. Given that many comments provided by respondents related to more than one question of inquiry within a single discussion, it was possible for a single section of text be present in more than one of the resulting MS Word files. Any comment that was not relevant to the research at hand was not coded, and therefore disregarded.

Each of the four new MS Word documents was then separately uploaded to Atlas.ti as a unique hermeneutic unit for coding and analysis. Each of these hermeneutic units was analyzed according to the following five step process.

- Pure Open Coding: Reviewing the text within each hermeneutic unit and coding each word or section of text in an approach consistent with Strauss and Corbin's micro-analysis recommendations (1998)
- First Level Data Reduction: Reviewing the results of the previous step to identify those codes that should obviously be combined based upon differences such as misspellings or word order
- Second Level Data Reduction: Reviewing the quotations associated with each coding label and then developing short definitions for each one. The resulting definitions for each code were then reviewed to identify those that seemed to be addressing the same phenomena, particularly in terms of skills, data, or perspectives used in that part of the strategy formulation process. Quotations for those codes were then reviewed, and code labels that appeared to address the same phenomena were combined and renamed appropriately
- Axial Coding: Developing an understanding of how the various codes within each hermeneutic unit related to each other. The first step in this process was developing more robust definitions for the remaining codes. Codes that seemed to address related processes were grouped into domains which are referred to as Code Families in Atlas.ti terminology. Once each domain was developed,

graphical representations of how the various processes represented by the codes within the domain related to each other were developed

- Selective Coding: Crafting descriptions of the observed phenomena so that the processes could be better understood and the new insights incorporated into the MDSM as appropriate

The following sections describe the outcomes of these efforts and the findings by each question of inquiry. Each section also includes graphical representations of how the new insights were incorporated into the MDSM.

Q₁: Competitor Information in the Strategy Formulation Process

How organizations react to competitive forces is one of the more prominently discussed topics related to the process of strategy formulation. It can be conceptualized as defining how the organization positions itself in relationship to its environment (Porter, 1980), taking a directly confrontational stance against competitors (Greenwald & Kahn, 2005), or finding ways to avoid direct competition with competitors (Kim & Mauborgne, 2005). While these three approaches each have different focuses, they are all premised on the organization's decisions being driven by the external environment. As can be seen in Figure 6, the organizations in this study appeared to be doing that by first gaining Competitive Insights and then engaging in a process that can be classified as Option Evaluation to determine how best to respond to those competitive forces in the environment.

Multi-Dimensional Strategy Model

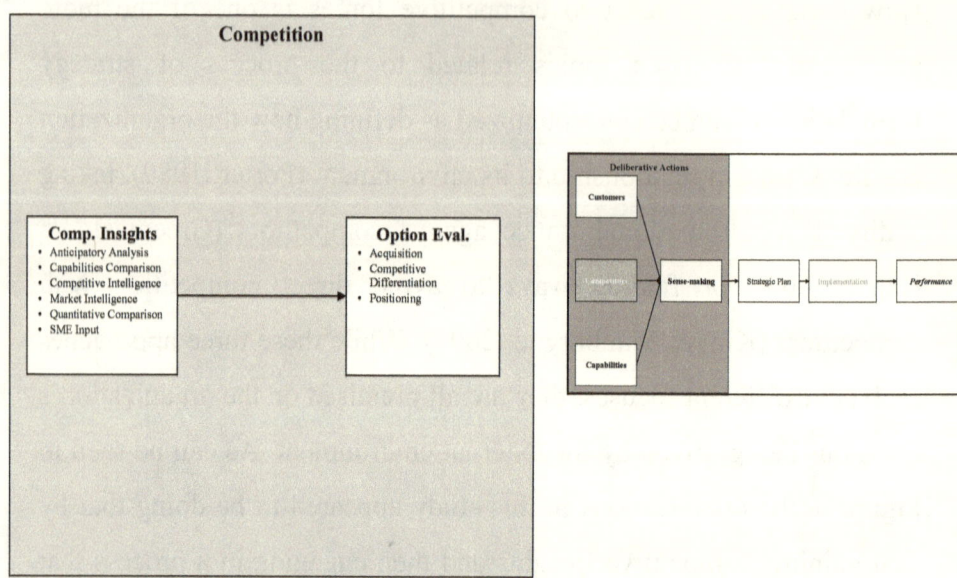

Figure 6. MDSM Competition Component

The Competitive Insights process appears to be focused on gathering data and understanding the various forces impacting the environment that the organization operates in. Based upon the feedback from the participants in this study, the approaches and data employed in these activities can be grouped into six categories:

- Anticipatory Analysis: Anticipating how the market may shift or change in the future, as well as competitors' reactions to those changes. Also includes anticipating competitors' reactions to the organization's own actions

- Capabilities Comparison: Comparing the organization to the competition based on the capabilities that can be leveraged for competitive advantage. - An outward focused capabilities analysis
- Competitive Intelligence: Actively gathering data about specific competitors so as to understand how their strategies, approaches and offerings compare to the organization conducting the strategic planning process. May be an ongoing effort or limited to a specific period of time
- Market Intelligence: Gathering and analyzing data about the broader market and the forces that may be effecting it rather than focusing on specific organizations that may be competing with the organization in question for resources, customers, or market share
- Quantitative Comparison: Comparing the organization to the competition based upon objective and quantifiable data. Includes both peer-to-peer comparisons as well as comparison to competitive benchmarks
- SME Input: Leveraging insights and inputs from individuals who have direct knowledge of the competition and what they may be doing beyond that of most individuals who are involved in the strategic planning process

Armed with these Competitive Insights, the organization must then make decisions about how it will, or will not, react to the forces that may be impacting it. This premise is similar to the idea behind Porter's Five-Forces (Porter, 1980), but the MDSM attempts to simplify the constructs of how and why organizations choose to respond to those forces by focusing on the three choices that organizations most often make in response to those challenges:

- Acquisition: Attempting to gain competitive advantage by acquiring new entities that add capabilities, offerings and/or customers rather than growing those advantages organically – Organic growth is address via development of capabilities
- Competitive Differentiation: Attempting to gain competitive advantage by focusing specifically on how the organization is different from its particular competitors
- Positioning: Determining the best place for the organization to place itself in the competitive market space. Can include both placing itself against competitors it feels it can effectively compete with, placing itself in a space where it can partner with complementary organizations, or placing itself in an *open space*

Interestingly, Positioning was discussed more often than either of the other possible approaches to responding to challenges in the competitive environment; although none of the three approaches were discussed at length by any of the respondents. While this could be a result of the questionnaire format, it could also be an artifact of the phenomenon that Collis observed where organizations tend to spend more time thinking about their strategies than working on how they are going to take action on those strategies (2005). Of particular note, however, is that this difference between inputs and decisions appears to be much more pronounced in relation to how organizations incorporate competition information into their strategy formulation processes than when they incorporate capabilities information.

Q₂: Capability Information in the Strategy Formulation Process

It has already been established that the ability to develop and leverage core capabilities is a key differentiator in an organization's success (Hamel & Prahalad, 1992; Hamel & Prahalad, 1994b; Prahalad & Hamel, 1990; Stalk et al., 1992; Ulrich & Smallwood, 2004; Vargo & Lusch, 2004). This inward looking approach is not discussed as often in the academic or popular business literature as externally focused approaches, but there is mounting evidence that some of the most successful organizations have achieved those outcomes by focusing first on what they do (Hamel & Prahalad, 1994a; Kim & Mauborgne, 1999; Scheraga, 2004). Moreover, this study found that the responding organizations indicated that they incorporate information about capabilities into their strategy formulation processes more often than they reported focusing on information about the competitive environment or customers. While using this information for strategy formulation is becoming more common, applying it to create business value can be challenging. The challenge is that developing these capabilities can be costly and time consuming. Organizations must seriously evaluate the value of those core competencies before making investment decisions (Hamel & Prahalad, 1989). As such, selecting the capabilities that the organization will focus on, and determining how they will be leveraged, are critical business decisions.

For the organizations that agreed to participate in this study, these decisions appear to start with an approach that can best be described as

Capability Selection, which is then followed by a determination of the best Execution Approach. Both of these processes are supported by a set of Rationales, through interactions similar to the process described in Figure 7.

Multi-Dimensional Strategy Model

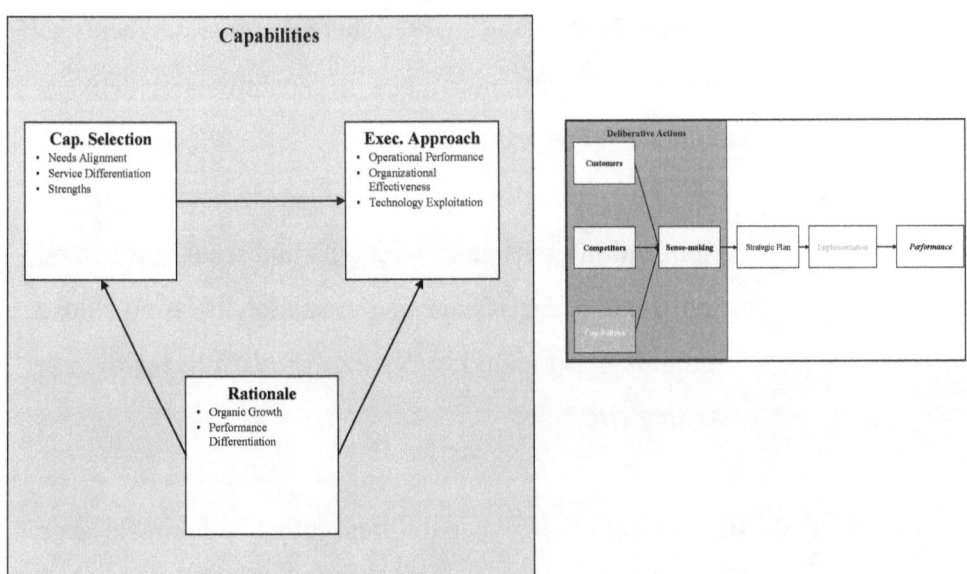

Figure 7. MDSM Capabilities Component

Capabilities Selection is where the organization decides what it is going to do. While the particular capabilities that are considered during this process can vary significantly from organization to organization, the approaches used to make these determinations tend to be based on the rationale that the selected capabilities should support one or more of three objectives:

- Needs Alignment: Developing a deep understanding of customer and market needs, and then aligning the organization's capabilities to be able to meet those needs in a markedly better way than other provider options
- Service Differentiation: Driving towards capabilities that meet the needs of a specific market segment, even at the risk of losing market share in other segments to whom those particular types of capabilities or delivery models may be less appealing
- Strengths: Developing a detailed understanding of the organization's particular strengths and weaknesses, and then looking for places in the market to apply those strengths. Also includes looking for ways to build upon existing strengths

Given that developing these capabilities often requires large investments, the participants in the strategy formulation process must be able to justify these decisions. This ability to justify these decisions is based upon the particular Rationale used to come to those conclusions. The outcome of this effort is often some sort of documentation chronicling why those particular capabilities were selected. For the organizations that participated in this study, there seemed to be two primary reasons why particular capabilities would be selected over others:

- Organic Growth: Choosing to drive the development and execution of specific capabilities because they can either increase current share of a particular market, allow the organization to move into a new market now, or grow in a new direction in the future
- Performance Differentiation: Choosing to drive the development and execution of specific capabilities because they allow the organization to deliver products or services that are sufficiently different from competitors

These rationales not only drive what the organization is going to do, but also greatly influence how the organization plans to go about its daily business. This decision process can be described as Execution Approach and may include three possible options:

- Operational Performance: Focusing on efficient and effective execution of core operations, and driving towards outcomes directly resulting from those activities. This includes not only excellence in current operations, but also continuously looking for ways to improve those activities and improve their outcomes
- Organizational Effectiveness: Focusing on leveraging organizational capabilities to drive strong performance. This includes both the macro level aspects, such as organizational culture, as well as more tactical

approaches such as human resources policies and hiring practices

- Technology Exploitation: Looking for ways to leverage new and advancing technologies to drive performance outcomes. This can include both technology for the sake of internal operations as well as differentiated technology to deliver services to the market

As with most approaches in the strategy formulation arena, these processes are not necessarily mutually exclusive, and any organization can choose to leverage one or more of these processes to varying degrees. A prime example of this is the earlier discussion of Wal-Mart who uses a Technology Exploitation approach to allow it to it to focus on Operational Excellence (Hamel & Prahalad, 1994b; Kim & Mauborgne, 1999; Scheraga, 2004). This is done to drive the outcomes necessary to execute a Needs Alignment with their capabilities to the needs of their customers.

Q₃: Customer Information in the Strategy Formulation Process

With the evolving customer management paradigm in business strategy literature (Kaplan & Norton, 2004), it is becoming more and more important to understand how organizations are integrating this information into their strategy formulation processes. A review of the responses of the organizations that participated in this study show that these activities tend to fit into three domains, Customer Insights, Market Insights, and Service Orientation. Customer Insights and Market Insights drive the organization's Service Orientation as illustrated in Figure 8.

Multi-Dimensional Strategy Model

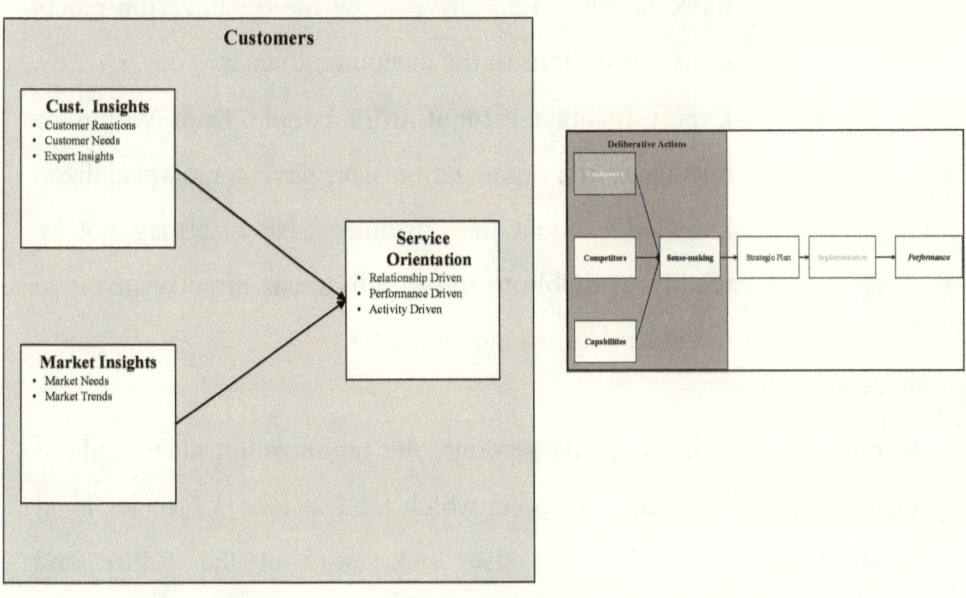

Figure 8. MDSM Customers Component

Customer Insights tend to be about understanding the customers who use and/or consume the products or services offered by the organization. It is much more focused than the Market Insights effort and tends to be based upon three types of data:

- Customer Reactions: Data about customers' behaviors and perceptions as a result of the actions the organization takes to try to serve them. – i.e., How the customer reacts to the organization and its efforts to meet their needs
- Customer Needs: Data about what the customers may need or want currently or at some time in the future, and what actions the organization may take to meet those needs. – i.e., Drives how the organization reacts to its perceptions of the customers' needs
- Expert Insights: Input from people from within or outside of the organization who have some specialized knowledge about the customer base that may not be readily available to those individuals directly involved in the strategic planning process

In conjunction with these data points, the organization also needs to take into account Market Insights which tend to take a broader level perspective. Market Insights also look more at the future and potentially unanticipated needs of the market place than does the

Customer Insights data. To do this, the Market Insights approach incorporates two categories of information:

- Market Needs: Data about the current state of the marketplace that may reveal needs of current and potential market segments that the organization could align itself to meet
- Market Trends: Data that enables understanding the direction and future position of the market so that the organization can anticipate changes that may need to be made to achieve advantage based on those shifts

Of course having Customer and Market Insights are useless unless the organization decides to do something with them. In this case, those decisions are defined as making determinations about what kind of Service Orientation the organization will adopt. The term Service Orientation here is consistent with the previously defined definition that looks at the collection of dynamics that allow an organization to effectively manage their customers (Bowen et al., 1989; Hogan et al., 1984). This definition differs from many of the existing definitions in that it specifically looks at Service Orientation as an organizational level issue rather than an individual level issue. The organizations that participated in this study tended to describe their Service Orientations in ways that could be classified into one of three categories:

- **Relationship Driven:** Aligning customer facing activities around how the organization interacts with and relates to its customers. Includes communication, service levels, and direct interaction levels
- **Performance Driven:** Aligning customer facing activities around outcome metrics associated with customer activities, and using those metrics as a primary tool to try to improve those activities
- **Activity Driven:** Specifically selecting particular activities to focus on based upon customer needs, and driving the organization's strategy and activities based on those decisions

This model is consistent with what has been seen in other organizations that were reviewed in the literature, such as Mobile NAM&R's and Harrah's attempts to integrate both Customer and Market Insights to refine their Service Orientations (Kaplan & Norton, 2001; Loveman, 2003; Sutton & Klein, 2003). In both cases, they leveraged understandings of Customer Needs and Market Needs to decide that they would be taking a more Relationship Driven approach that was enabled by an Activity Driven approach that focused on how they were going to treat specific customers in specific ways. Of course both of these examples involved an integration of this new customer perspective with an understanding of the organization's capabilities. The process for developing an integrated understanding of these perspectives is the topic of the next section.

Q₄: **Sense-making in the Strategy Formulation Process**

Sense-making is about understanding how individuals in organizations attempt to explain sets of clues from their environment and then make appropriate decisions based on that data (Maitlis, 2005). The value of sense-making as a topic in the strategy formulation discussion is that there is growing evidence that it has a direct link to organizational outcomes (Maitlis, 2005; Thomas et al., 1993). Based upon the comments provided by the participants in this study, the processes that organizations use when trying to make sense of the various data and inputs during the strategy formulation process can be conceptualized into two sets of activities and two sets of influencers. Data Reduction and Decision Techniques are the mechanisms of the activities. Data Reduction is used to make determinations about what kinds of information the organization will include and exclude in their strategy formulation processes. Decision Techniques are the ways that selected data is manipulated so that the organization can reach conclusions and/or consensus about the most appropriate courses of action. The Organizational Orientation is a strategic influencer of these activities, while Process Preference is more of a tactical influencer. Figure 9 illustrates these relationships.

Multi-Dimensional Strategy Model

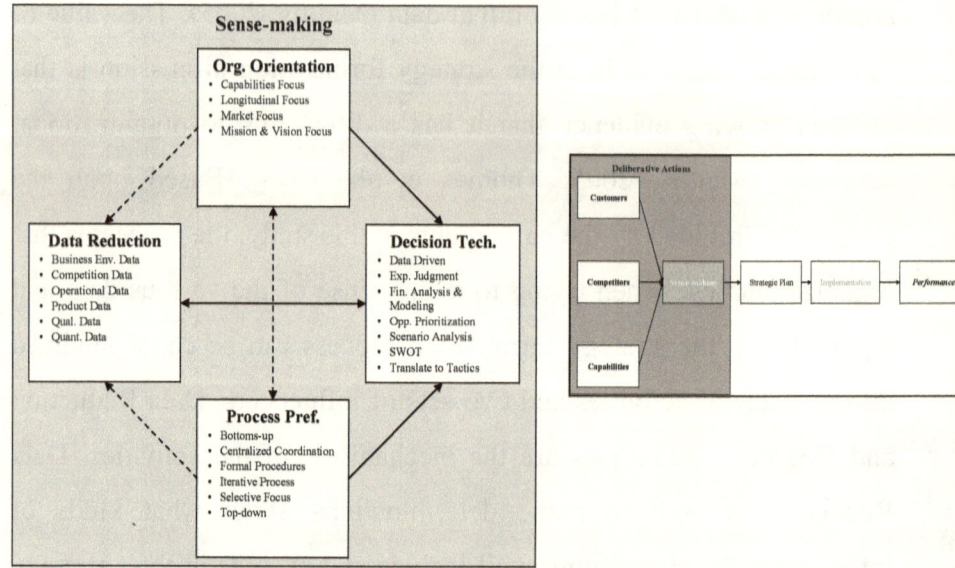

Figure 9. MDSM Sense-making Component

Data reduction processes are specifically focused on selecting and deselecting information from both internal and external sources. Much of this data is drawn from the outputs of the previously described efforts related to the incorporation of customers, capabilities, and competitors into the strategy formulation process. This is very much related to the Scanning variable in Thomas, Clark and Giola's sense-making model (1993); except that where that model takes a much broader perspective to sense-making within the organization, the MDSM is much more focused on strategic decisions. This conclusion is illustrated by the six kinds of data that seem to be most common in these activities:

- Business Environment Data: Data obtained through a macro view of the overall environment in which the organization operates. The goal is to understand how any changes to that environment do or could potentially impact the organization
- Competition Data: Data specifically focused around the behavior and/or offerings of other organizations that could compete against the organization for customers, resources or market share
- Operational Data: Data focused on operational inputs and outputs over some period of time. Goal is to understand how the organization is driving towards desired outcomes
- Product Data: Data about the particular products the organization is bringing to the market and how they can be leveraged to better serve the market
- Qualitative Data: Data based on information and insights of a more subjective nature (i.e., cannot be directly quantified) that may be integrated into the strategic planning process
- Quantitative Data: Data based on information and insights of a more objective nature (i.e., can be directly

quantified) that may be integrated into the strategic planning process

Once decisions are made about what kinds of data will be included in the strategy formulation efforts, the organization must then decide how that data will be used. While Data Reduction and selection of particular Decision Techniques do appear to be mutually influential processes, the outcomes of the Data Reduction efforts appear to be driving the selection of particular Decision Techniques more so than preferences for particular Decision Techniques appear to be driving Data Reduction decisions. Whether this is an issue of data availability or an artifact of previous efforts influencing future decisions was not explored in this study, but such a question would be an excellent foundation for subsequent research. Those issues notwithstanding, the kinds of Decision Techniques described by participants in this study can be grouped into one of seven approaches:

- Data Driven: Approaches that are primarily focused on using available information (qualitative or quantitative) to understand how factors represented by that data could/do impact the organization
- Experiential Judgment: Approaches that are primarily based on experiences and intuition of individual(s) involved in the strategic planning process. Tends to leverage qualitative data more than quantitative data

- Financial Analysis and Modeling: Approaches that rely more on financial modeling and pro forma analysis (e.g., profitability, net income) as the primary catalyst for decision making
- Opportunity Prioritization: Approaches that focus on ranking potential opportunities based on some set of criteria, and then basing which opportunities the organization will pursue on those rankings
- Scenario Analysis: Approaches that focus on crafting various scenarios that describe potential outcomes based on some predefined and documented assumptions, and then basing decisions on an evaluation of the predicted outcomes of those possible scenarios
- SWOT: Approaches that focus on documenting the organization's Strengths, Weaknesses, Opportunities, and Threats and then using that data to determine the best course of action. May also include approaches that are more biased towards a purely strengths based paradigm
- Translate to Tactics: Approaches that take broad strategic directives and then quickly move to definition of tactics and feasibility of those tactics to determine which options are most appropriate

These various techniques are similar to the Interpretation and Action phases of Thomas, Clark and Giola's sense-making model (1993), but again that model appears to be looking more at broad cognitive processes within an organization rather than understanding how the organization drives the outcomes of the strategic planning process. Also of note is that the techniques described in the MDSM could be used to varying degrees during different parts of the strategy formulation process. The organization's decisions about which techniques to use, and when they would be most appropriate, appeared to be largely a function of the reporting organization's Organizational Orientation and Process Preference.

Organizational Orientation is related to understanding how the organization sees itself, its environment, and how it wants to be viewed by others. It is the predominant mental model that the organization uses to understand how it fits into the broader world. Like all mental models, it drives not only how the organization makes sense of the world, but also how it chooses to take action (Senge, 1994). These models tend to be driven by four focuses:

- Capabilities Focus: Focusing primarily on the organization's internal capabilities and allowing that perspective to significantly impact the assumptions and decisions of the strategic planning process
- Longitudinal Focus: Taking a multi-year view of the organization that both integrates where the organization

has been (i.e., historical performance) and where it wants to be over the next several years (e.g., 3-5 years) and allowing that perspective to significantly impact the assumptions and decisions of the strategic planning process

- Market Focused: Maintaining awareness of external market changes and potential evolving trends and allowing that perspective to significantly impact the assumptions and decisions of the strategic planning process
- Mission & Vision Focus: Aligning strategic planning efforts around the organization's mission and vision (i.e., *why we are here*) and allowing that perspective to significantly impact the assumptions and decisions in the strategic planning process

These focuses are neither mutually exclusive, nor necessarily dependent. The degree to which an organization is Capabilities Focused does not preclude it from also being Market Focused. What it does mean, however, is that the organization will select data and decision techniques that allow it to be simultaneously internally and externally focused. The decisions of particular data and techniques selected tend to be driven by the organization's Process Preference.

Whereas the Organizational Orientation is more about the mental models the organization is using, the Process Preference is about how the organization chooses to get things done. Future research may find that alignment between an organization's Process Preference for strategy formulation and other activities is a critical factor in the success of strategy implementation, but that question was not addressed here and there is no supporting evidence directly related to that assertion at this time. What the current evidence does support is that Process Preferences can be classified into one of six categories:

- Bottoms-up: Driving the strategic planning process by developing goals, objectives, and plans at the operating units and then integrating those plans into larger overall plans that then drive the larger organization
- Centralized Coordination: Management of strategic planning activities by a dedicated functional unit or group of resources that exist as an established on-going entity rather than an ad hoc group that exists for a finite period of time, and may or may not include the same individuals at a later date
- Formal Procedures: Management of the strategy formulation process through formal and prescriptive procedures to develop those plans. May include prescribed repeatable steps, a predetermined format for the strategic planning output, and/or establishment of a specific time and/or place where strategic issues are discussed and plans developed

- Iterative Process: Management of the strategy formulation process through multiple rounds of review and revision by a wide variety of stakeholders and subject matter experts
- Selective Focus: Processes that keep the organization focused on particular area(s) that are of critical importance to their business during analysis efforts. Objective is to not loose sight of what is important to maintaining organizational success
- Top-Down: Driving the strategic planning process by having senior leaders within the organization (e.g., CEO, Board of Directors, Senior Management Team) come to agreement about the organization's goals and objectives, then promulgating those goals and objectives out to the rest of the organization

The categories of Centralized Coordination, Formal Procedures, Iterative Processes, and Selective Focus all tend to be non-mutually exclusive continuums; while it appears that Bottoms-up and Top-down approaches are mutually exclusive sides of the same continuum. The main reason for keeping the Bottoms-up and Top-down approaches separated is that the techniques and perspectives used in each one appear to be sufficiently different to warrant separate classifications. It should be noted, however, that the Top-down approach appears to be the more common among the responses from participants in this study, and is more consistent with the descriptions in the literature at large.

Finalized Multi-Dimensional Strategy Model

Now that the hypotheses for this research study have been retained, and the qualitative analysis phase has been completed, the finalized Multi-Dimensional Strategy Model (MDSM) can be presented with confidence that it does represent the strategy formulation processes of top performing organizations, or at least the strategy formulation processes of the organizations that agreed to participate in this study. Figure 10 presents this updated model.

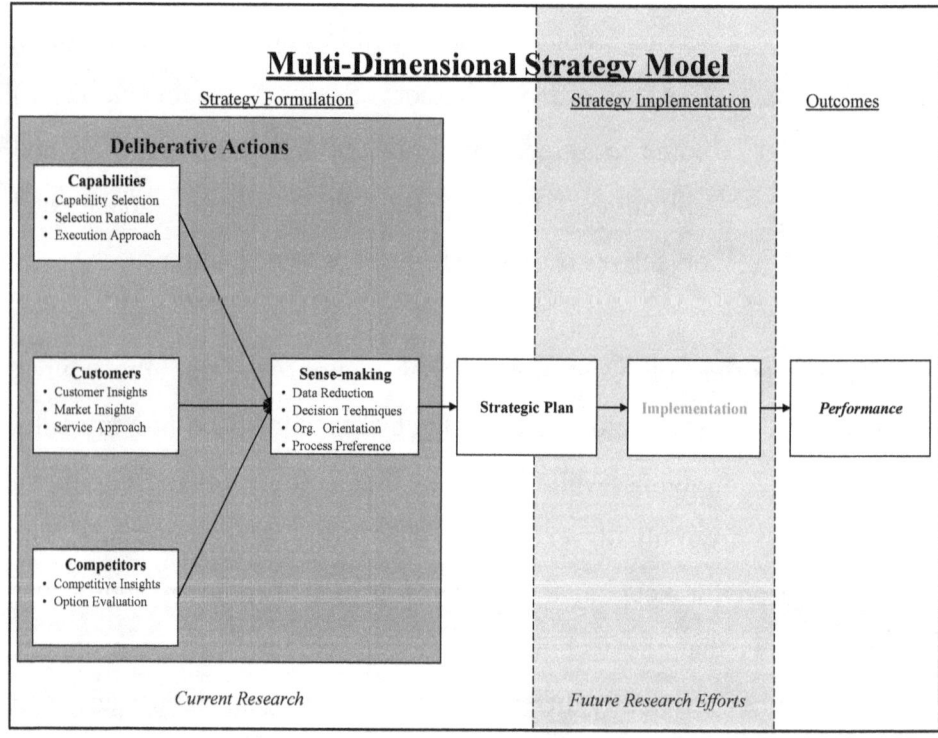

Figure 10. Updated Multi-Dimensional Strategy Model

The updated model is largely consistent with the model originally proposed in Figure 1 of this report. The primary enhancements are the addition of the domains that were found to be present within the Capabilities, Customer, Competitors, and Sense-making components of the model; as well as the reordering of Capabilities, Customers, and Competitors from top to bottom in the Deliberative Action box. This was done to reflect the higher degree of incorporation of these components into the strategy formulation process based on the mean ratings from the participants in this study. The implications and applications of this model are discussed in the closing section of this report.

Implications & Application

This study has been an attempt to answer one very simple research question:

Do organizations that take an approach to strategy formulation that is consistent with a model based on a systems thinking perspective perform better than the overall market?

The Multi-Dimensional Strategy Model that was developed during this study has been found to be consistent with reality, or at least reality as it is represented by the responses of the organizations that participated in this study. The aggregate responses of the participating organizations showed that they do indeed use approaches similar to the MDSM in their strategy formulation processes, even if they do not classify those efforts as such. Even so, the question that must also be asked is this model can indeed be used to help drive organizational improvement and performance? While this study did not specifically measure performance and improvement outcomes, it did control for that variable by limiting study participation to only organizations that met one of two high performance criteria. Moreover, the study also assessed participants' perceptions of the strategy formulation processes' impact on their organizations' performance. An overwhelming number of participants reported that they did perceive the outcomes of their strategy formulation efforts as having a positive impact on their organizations' performance. Given these data points, it can be assumed that there is a high likelihood that the MDSM could have a positive impact on the performance outcomes of organizations that choose to utilize it in their strategy formulation efforts.

This study also included a qualitative phase that was focused on the identification of commonalities within the Capabilities, Customers, Competition, and Sense-making components of the MDSM. For the Capabilities, Customers, and Competitors components; the main outcomes were three sub-models of the MDSM that provide linear conceptualizations of how organizations gather information and come to conclusions regarding these three constructs so that they can be incorporated into the strategy formulation process. While each model is unique, they all begin with how the organizations collect and collate the data relative to those constructs, and then conclude with how the organizations develop understandings of the impacts of those drivers. These new sub-models are useful from an academic perspective because they represent deeper dives on the topics, so as to help promote simplification of these ideas for the sake of study and understanding. The sub-models are also useful from a practical perspective because they clearly describe the assumptions and generalizations that managers need to be able to take into account when incorporating these domains in their strategy formulation activities. Among other benefits, this allows managers to address Porter's admonition that organizations must plunge below the surface level understandings of the forces that are impacting them if they want to be successful (1980). Having these understandings, however, is not much use unless the organization can make sense of that information so that appropriate business decisions can be made.

As already discussed, the sense-making process is a key driver of organizational outcomes (Maitlis, 2005; Thomas et al., 1993), but there is currently a dearth of models that directly address this construct as it relates to strategy formulation processes (Brown, 2006). As a result, the sense-making process in most organizations tends to occur through intuitive synthesis (Khatri, 1994), or experiential judgment as it was described in this study. Experiential judgment based process are rarely the most effective option. A model that describes this process could help drive more efficient efforts, but up to this time there have not been any published efforts specifically focused on sense-making as it applies to strategy formulation. The qualitative analysis phase of this study included the development of a sub-model of the MDSM that begins to address that deficiency. In simplest terms, the sense-making process is about understanding how organizations first decide what data they will include in, and exclude from, their strategy formulation processes, and then what techniques they will chose to use to manipulate that data to come to decisions. The selection of data and techniques is typically driven by both the organizational and tactical orientations of the organization in question. Once an organization better understands their own orientations, they can focus less energy on technique selection, and more on appropriate decision making activities.

While there is still additional work that could be done relative to the extension and expansion of the concepts inherent in the MDSM, the data presented here supports the assertion that organizations that use a systems thinking based approach for strategy formulation are more likely to be successful than those that do not. While the presentation of this idea in a coherent model that is built upon academic rigor is a novel concept, many successful managers have learned from experience to apply similar approaches. In the absence of the opportunity to learn via this modality, however, a model like the MDSM could provide a way for managers without that level of seasoning to understand how to better negotiate this process. In particular, it helps them understand the level of focus required, what kinds of data to incorporate, and how to make sense of the mounds of information and inputs that are present during these efforts. When properly leveraged, these insights will enable these managers to more effectively answer the questions of how to make their organizations more successful.

List of Figures

Figure 1. Multi-Dimensional Strategy Model 33
Figure 2. Research Model 40
Figure 3. Hypotheses Alignment to MDSM 41
Figure 4. MDMS and Questions of Inquiry 44
Figure 5. Questionnaire Response Histogram 66
Figure 6. MDSM Competition Component 76
Figure 7. MDSM Capabilities Component 81
Figure 8. MDSM Customers Component 85
Figure 9. MDSM Sense-making Component 90
Figure 10. Updated Multi-Dimensional Strategy Model 98

List of Tables

Table 1. Data Collection Response Rates 57
Table 2. Overall Demographic Comparisons 60
Table 3. Top 200 Organizations Demographic Comparison 62
Table 4. Fortune 500 Organizations Demographic Comparison 63
Table 5. Data to Hypothesis linkage 65
Table 6. Means and Standard Deviations 67
Table 7. Chi – Squared Calculations 69

References

Argyres, N., & McGahan, A. M. (2002). An interview with Michael Porter. *Academy of Management Executive, 16,* 41-42.

Bhattacharya, C. B. & Sen, S. (2003). Consumer-company identification: A framework for understanding consumers' relationships with companies. *Journal of Marketing, 67,* 76-88.

Bowen, D. E., Siehl, C., & Schneider, B. (1989). A framework for analyzing customer service orientations in manufacturing. *Academy of Management Review, 14,* 75-96.

Brown, J. (2006). Application of an OD perspective to develop a new model of the strategy formulation process. *The Business Review, Cambridge, 6,* 26-31.

Chalmers, A. F. (1999). *What is this thing called science.* Indianapolis, IN: Hackett Publishing Company, Inc.

Church, A. H., & Waclawski, J. (1998). *Designing and using organizational surveys.* San Francisco: Jossey-Bass.

Collins, J. (2001). *Good to great.* New York: HarperBusiness.

Collins, J., & Porras, J. I. (2002). *Built to last.* New York: Collins Business Essentials.

Collis, D. J. (2005). *Strategy: Create and implement the best strategy for your business.* Boston: Harvard Business School Press.

Collis, D. J., & Montgomery, C. A. (1995). Competing on resources: Strategy in the 1990s. *Harvard Business Review, 73,* 118-128.

Cooperrider, D. L., & Sekerka, L. E. (2003). Toward a theory of positive organizational change. In K. S. Cameron, J. E. Dutton, & R. E. Quinn (Eds.), *Positive organizational scholarship* (pp. 225-240). San Francisco: Berrett-Koehler Publishers, Inc.

Creswell, J. W. (2003). *Research design* (2nd ed.). Thousand Oaks, CA: Sage Publications.

Cummings, S., & Angwin, D. (2004). The future shape of strategy: Lemmings or chimeras? *Academy of Management Executive, 18,* 21-36.

Cummings, T. G., & Worley, C. G. (2005). *Organization development and change* (8th ed.). Mason, OH: Thomas South-Western.

Dean, J. W., & Sharfman, M. P. (1996). Does decision process matter? A study of strategic decision-making effectiveness. *Academy of Management Journal, 39,* 368-396.

Epstein, M. J., & Westbrook, R. A. (2001). Linking actions to profits in strategic decision making. *MIT Sloan Management Review, 42,* 39-49.

French, W. L., & Bell, C. H. (1999). *Organization development* (6th ed.). Upper Saddle River, NJ: Prentice-Hall, Inc.

Garvin, D. A. (1991). How the Baldridge Award really works. *Harvard Business Review, 69,* 80-93.

Giola, D. A., Thomas, J. B., Clark, S. M., & Chittipeddi, K. (1994). Symbolism and strategic change in academia: The dynamics of sensemaking and influence. *Organizational Science, 5,* 363-383.

Gittell, J. H. (2001). Investing in relationships. *Harvard Business Review, 79,* 28-30.

Greenwald, B., & Kahn, J. (2005). *Competition demystified.* New York: Penguin Group.

Griffith, S. B. (1963). *Sun Tzu the art of war.* London: Oxford University Press.

Grimm, L. G. (1993). *Statistical applications for the behavioral sciences.* New York: John Wiley & Sons, Inc.

Gulati, R., & Oldroyd, J. B. (2005). The quest for customer focus. *Harvard Business Review, 83,* 92-101.

Gupta, A. K. (1980). *The process of strategy formulation: A descriptive analysis.* Boston: Harvard University.

Hamel, G. (1996). Strategy as revolution. *Harvard Business Review, 74,* 69-82.

Hamel, G., & Prahalad, C. K. (1989). Strategic intent. *Harvard Business Review, 67,* 63-78.

Hamel, G., & Prahalad, C. K. (1992). Capabilities-based competition. *Harvard Business Review, 70,* 164-170.

Hamel, G., & Prahalad, C. K. (1994a). *Competing for the future.* Boston: Harvard Business School Press.

Hamel, G., & Prahalad, C. K. (1994b). Competing for the future. *Harvard Business Review, 72,* 122-128.

Hansen, G. S., & Wernerfelt, B. (1989). Determinants of firm performance: The relative importance of economic and organizational factors. *Strategic Management Journal, 10,* 399-411.

Harrington, R. J., Lemak, D. J., Reed, R., & Kendall, K. W. (2004). A question of fit: The links among environment, strategy formulation, and performance. *Journal of Business & Management, 10,* 15-38.

Hart, S. L., & Milstein, M. B. (1999). Global sustainability and the creative destruction of industries. *Sloan Management Review, 41,* 23-33.

Hatch, M. J. (1997). *Organization theory.* New York: Oxford University Press.

Hogan, J., Hogan, R., & Busch, C. M. (1984). How to measure service orientation. *Journal of Applied Psychology, 69,* 167-173.

Hrebinaik, L. G., & Joyce, W. F. (2001). Implementing strategy: An appraisal and agenda for future research. In M. A. Hitt, R. E. Freeman, & J. S. Harrison (Eds.), *Handbook of strategic management* (pp. 602-626). Oxford, England: Blackwell Publishing, Ltd.

Iacobucci, D. (1996). The quality improvement customers didn't want. *Harvard Business Review, 74,* 20-25.

Johnson, L. K. (2002). The real value of customer loyalty. *MIT Sloan Management Review, 43,* 14-17.

Kaplan, R. S., & Norton, D. P. (2001). *The strategy-focused organization.* Boston: Harvard Business School Press.

Kaplan, R. S., & Norton, D. P. (2004). *Strategy maps.* Boston: Harvard Business School Press.

Kerlinger, F. N., & Lee, H. B. (2000). *Foundations of behavioral research.* (Fourth Edition ed.) Toronto, ON: Wadsworth.

Khatri, N. (1994). *Strategic processes and organizational performance.* New York: State University of New York.

Kim, W. C., & Mauborgne, R. (1999). Strategy, value innovation, and the knowledge economy. *Sloan Management Review, 40,* 41-54.

Kim, W. C., & Mauborgne, R. (2005). *Blue ocean strategy.* Boston: Harvard Business School Press.

Kirby, J. (2005). Toward a theory of high performance. *Harvard Business Review, 83,* 30-39.

Kuhn, T. S. (1996). *The structure of scientific revolutions.* Chicago: The University of Chicago Press.

Leath, B. (2007). *Cultivating the strategic mind.* Indianapolis: IBJ Custom Publishing.

Loveman, G. (2003). Diamonds in the data mine. *Harvard Business Review, 81,* 109-113.

Luehrman, T. A. (1998). Strategy as a portfolio of real options. *Harvard Business Review, 76,* 89-99.

Maitlis, S. (2005). The social processes of organizational sensemaking. *Academy of Management Journal, 48,* 21-49.

Mintzberg, H. (1987). Crafting strategy. *Harvard Business Review, 65,* 66-75.

Mintzberg, H. (1994). *The rise and fall of strategic planning.* Boston: Harvard Business School Press.

Nicholas, J. M., & Katz, M. (1985). Research methods and reporting practices in organization development: A review and some guidelines. *Academy of Management Review, 10,* 737-749.

Panayides, P. M. (2004). Logistics service providers: an empirical study of marketing strategies and company performance. *International Journal of Logistics: Research & Applications, 7,* 1-15.

Peters, T. (2001). Tom Peters's true confessions. *Fast Company,* 78-92.

Pophan, W. J., & Sirotnik, K. A. (1992). *Understanding statistics in education.* Itasca, IL: F. E. Peacock Publishers, Inc.

Porter, M. E. (1980). *Competitive strategy.* New York: The Free Press.

Porter, M. E. (1996). What is strategy? *Harvard Business Review, 74,* 61-78.

Porter, M. E. (1998). Clusters and the new economics of competition. *Harvard Business Review, 76,* 77-90.

Porter, M. E. (2001). Strategy and the internet. *Harvard Business Review, 79,* 62-78.

Prahalad, C. K., & Hamel, G. (1990). The core competence of the corporation. *Harvard Business Review, 68,* 79-91.

Prokesch, S. E. (1995). Competing on customer service: An interview with British Airways' Sir Colin Marshall. *Harvard Business Review, 73,* 100-112.

Ramanujam, V., Venkatraman, N., & Camillus, J. C. (1986). Multi-objective assessment of effectiveness of strategic planning: A discriminant analysis approach. *Academy of Management Journal, 29,* 347-372.

Rucci, A. J., Kirn, S. P., & Quinn, R. T. (1998). The employee-customer-profit chain at Sears. *Harvard Business Review, 76,* 82-97.

Rudestam, K. E., & Newton, R. R. (2001). *Surviving your dissertation* (2nd ed.). Thousand Oaks, CA: Sage Publications, Inc.

Scheraga, D. (2004). What makes Wal-Mart tick. *Chain Store Age, 80,* 49-50.

Senge, P. M. (1994). *The fifth discipline.* New York: Currency Doubleday.

Silbiger, S. (1999). *The ten day MBA* (Rev. ed.). New York: Quill William Morrow.

Stalk, G., Evans, P., & Shulman, L. E. (1992). Competing on capabilities: The new rules of corporate strategy. *Harvard Business Review, 70,* 54-66.

Stone, E. (1978). *Research methods in organizational behavior.* Santa Monica, CA: Good Year Publishing Company.

Strauss, A., & Corbin, J. (1998). *Basics of qualitative research* (2nd ed.). Thousand Oaks, CA: Sage Publications.

Sutton, D., & Klein, T. (2003). *Enterprise marketing management.* Hoboken, NJ: John Wiley & Sons, Inc.

Thomas, J. B., Clark, S. M., & Giola, D. A. (1993). Strategic sensemaking and organizational performance: Linkages among scanning, interpretation, action, and outcomes. *Academy of Management Journal, 36,* 239-270.

Ulrich, D., & Smallwood, N. (2004). Capitalizing on capabilities. *Harvard Business Review, 82,* 119-127.

Urban, G. L. (2004). The emerging era of customer advocacy. *MIT Sloan Management Review, 45,* 77-82.

Vandermerwe, S. (2000). How increasing value to customers improves business results. *Sloan Management Review, 42,* 27-37.

Vargo, S. L., & Lusch, R. F. (2004). Evolving to a new dominant logic for marketing. *Journal of Marketing, 68,* 1-17.

Viguerie, S. P., & Thompson, C. (2005). The faster they fall. *Harvard Business Review, 83,* 22.

Watson, A., & Wooldridge, B. (2005). Business unit manager influence on corporate-level strategy formulation. *Journal of Managerial Issues, 17,* 147-161.

Welcome to CRSP (2006). Retrieved May 22, 2006, from http://www.crsp.com

Wilson, H., Daniel, E., & McDonald, M. (2002). Factors for success in customer relationship management (CRM) systems. *Journal of Marketing Management, 18,* 193-219.

Worley, C. G., Hitchin, D. E., & Ross, W. R. (1996). *Integrated strategic change.* Reading, MA: Addison-Wesley Publishing Company.

About the Author

Jimmy Brown, Ph.D., is a consultant; coach and author with more than 14 years of experience helping organizations and individuals achieve peak performance. During his career, Dr. Brown has worked around the globe and held senior level consulting positions at several marquee firms. He is a frequent author and conference speaker on the topics of business strategy, organizational change, and peak personal performance, including delivery of the key note address at the 2006 Global Business and Finance Research Conference in London. Dr. Brown is an adjunct professor at several universities' psychology and management programs, and is regularly sought out for his insights on how to practically apply cutting edge theory to solving real world problems. He can be reached via his website at www.3cstrategy.com.

www.ingramcontent.com/pod-product-compliance
Lightning Source LLC
Chambersburg PA
CBHW022020170526
45157CB00003B/1309